# *Mysteries from the Dawn of Time*

In the beauty of an ancient artifact, in the majesty of a monument from a distant past, we sense the living, vibrant soul of a people who still have much to teach us today. Despite all of our technological and material gains, we long for the spiritual strength and grace that was theirs.

*Ancient Teachings for Beginners* reaches across the ages and uncovers the metaphysical wisdom of our venerable ancestors. But it is much more than a history lesson—it is a practical guidebook for applying this knowledge to the development of your psychic abilities and the unfoldment of your spiritual potential.

Applying the lessons and techniques in this book, you will reclaim your inner power to move freely between all worlds, and all times.

## About the Author

Douglas De Long is a spiritual/personal counselor, past life therapist, and chakra master. He has studied and developed his own psychic abilities and spiritual growth for over twenty years. He created a unique course that he has been teaching for more than five years. He has been guided to put his knowledge and channeled teachings into book form in order to help humankind open up and develop their innate abilities.

Douglas and his wife, Carol, reside in Saskatoon, Saskatchewan where they own and operate the De Long Ancient Mystery School.

## To Write to the Author

If you wish to contact the author or would like more information about this book, you may write to the author in care of Llewellyn Worldwide, and we will forward your request. Both the author and the publisher appreciate hearing from you and learning of your enjoyment of this book and how it has helped you. Llewellyn Worldwide cannot guarantee that every letter written to the author can be answered, but all will be forwarded. Please write to:

Douglas De Long
℅ Llewellyn Worldwide, Ltd.
P.O. Box 64383, Dept. K214-3
St. Paul, MN 55164-0383, U.S.A.

Please enclose a self-addressed, stamped envelope for reply,
or $1.00 to cover costs. If outside U.S.A., enclose international
postal reply coupon.

# ANCIENT
# TEACHINGS
# *for* BEGINNERS

- *Auras* • *Chakras* • *Angels*
- *Rebirth* • *Astral Projection*

## Douglas De Long

2000
Llewellyn Publications
St. Paul, Minnesota, 55164-0383, U.S.A.

FIRST EDITION
Second Printing, 2000

Cover design by Lisa Novak
Editing and interior design by Tom Lewis
Interior illustrations by William Merlin Cannon

Library of Congress Cataloging-in-Publication Data

De Long, Douglas, 1954-
    Ancient teachings for beginners : a course in psychic and spritual
    development / Douglas De Long.-- 1st ed.
        p. cm.
    Includes bibliographical references.
    ISBN: 1-56718-214-3
    1. Hermetism. I. Title.

BF1611 .D325 2000
133'.45--dc21

00-35235

The practices, techniques, and exercises described in this book should not be used as an alternative to professional medical diagnosis or treatment. The author and publisher of this book are not responsible in any manner whatsoever for any injury or negative effects that may occur through following the instructions and advice contained herein. It is recommended that you consult your medical professional to determine whether you should undertake any course of practice before beginning any treatment or technique discussed in this book.

Llewellyn Worldwide does not participate in, endorse, or have any authority or responsibility concerning private business transactions between our authors and the public.
    All mail addressed to the author is forwarded but the publisher cannot, unless specifically instructed by the author, give out an address or phone number.
                Llewellyn Publications
                A Division of Llewellyn Worldwide, Ltd.
                P.O. Box 64383, Dept. K214-3
                St. Paul, Minnesota 55164-0383, U.S.A.
                www.llewellyn.com

Printed in the United States of America

*Dedicated to Carol, my wife and soulmate,*
*and to my heavenly messengers and spirit guides*

# Contents

Introduction . . . . . . . . . . . . . . . . . . . . . . . . . . . . . . . . . . .ix

1 A Brief History of the Ancient Mystery
   Schools and Religions . . . . . . . . . . . . . . .1

2 The Third Eye Chakra . . . . . . . . . . . . . . .23

3 The Crown Chakra . . . . . . . . . . . . . . . . . .37

4 The Human Aura . . . . . . . . . . . . . . . . . . .51

5 Reading and Interpreting
   the Human Aura . . . . . . . . . . . . . . . . . . .79

6 The Chakra System . . . . . . . . . . . . . . . . . .97

7 Kundalini and Chakra Energy for
   Healing and Enlightenment . . . . . . . .137

8 Channeling: Working With Your
   Angels and Spirit Guides . . . . . . . . . .161

9 Astral Projection . . . . . . . . . . . . . . . . . . .201

10 Reincarnation . . . . . . . . . . . . . . . . . . . . .211

11 The Master's Last Days . . . . . . . . . . . . .221

viii    Contents

Appendix 1 ....................................233

Appendix 2 ...................................235

Appendix 3 ...................................239

Endnotes ....................................241

Bibliography ................................243

Index ......................................245

# Introduction

*Ancient Teachings for Beginners* is a detailed and intense course in psychic development and spiritual growth with exercises and experiments designed to lead you to your full psychic potential. Using the proven methods in this book, you will enhance your psychic abilities and create a more awakened you.

All of us possess some psychic abilities. Through this course, you will be able to tap into your true gifts. You can become clairvoyant, clairaudient, clairsentient, learn to see the human aura and interpret its colors, meet and communicate with your angels and spirit guides, work as a healer using Universal Energy or as a gifted teacher or counselor. This unique course gives you the instructions and understanding needed to enhance your psychic abilities that are hidden within. These wonderful gifts are yours to use to help yourself and others. We all have a purpose in life, a reason for being here. Hopefully, you will gain insight into your life's purpose to help make a difference.

It is my utmost desire and wish for all of you to reach your goals and assist humankind. Let's make this a better world. After all, we are all here to serve one another.

May love and the light of the angels be with you.

# Chapter 1

# *A Brief History of the Ancient Mystery Schools and Religions*

The noblest employment of the mind of man is
the study of the works of his creator.
—*Unto Thee I Grant*

The modern world is full of technology: computers, telecommunications, jet aircraft for world travel, fancy land vehicles, huge buildings within large urban centers, and mass marketing for all our everyday needs. This may seem like the "age of wonders," but is it really?

The modern world is materialistic and stressful. In many families, both parents work just to maintain a comfortable standard of living. Stress has become the major problem for many people. Many school-age children are being medicated just to keep them calm and orderly while attending school.

Fortunately, many individuals are seeking something more than mere materialism: a higher purpose to their lives. People are awakening and becoming more spiritual. As these people raise their consciousness to higher levels of awareness, the world will change. They are attuning to the higher energy vibrations that emanate from the God source, and in so doing they are helping others. If this continues, perhaps our beautiful planet will survive.

## The Ancient Mystery Schools

In ancient times, the human race was more attuned to nature, to the spiritual, and to the psychic. There was more of an acceptance of the psychic realm. For many, it was a way of life.

In antiquity, there were ancient mystery schools and healing centers where initiates were taught the secrets and mysteries of life. Some of the teachings were dedicated to the study and proper use of natural healing energies both within and outside of the human body. There is a universal healing energy, a life force that exists in all of nature. Because this natural energy vibrates at a very high frequency, most people cannot sense it. The universal healing energy can be brought into a human body where it activates the body's own life force and healing energy. Students or initiates were trained in ancient healing techniques, taught to see the human aura or energy field, and to interpret the meanings of the colors within the aura. Beyond these skills, they were encouraged to develop their psychic abilities and were ultimately placed on a spiritual path dedicated to the service of others.

## From Atlantis to Egypt

There was a major civilization that predated Egypt by several thousand years: this was the mystical land of Atlantis. The ancient mystery and healing schools began there. These schools or centers of education were located throughout the land, where some were found in mountainous regions. The Greek philosopher Plato (circa 400 B.C.E.) makes reference to Atlantis in two of his dialogues, *Timaeus* and *Critias*. In his

1882 book, *Atlantis: The Antediluvian World*, former U.S. senator Ignatius Donnelly referred to the Azores Islands in the eastern Atlantic Ocean as the site of Atlantis. In fact, the Azores Islands still contain evidence that reveals precisely where Atlanteans performed their sacred rituals.

Prior to the final destruction of the island continent of Atlantis, groups of Atlanteans, or Atlantans, established colonies in South America and in the Nile valley of Egypt. According to Edgar Cayce, who was known as America's "sleeping prophet," Atlantean leaders prepared a portion of the population for emigration to preserve the civilization in the event of the predicted destruction of Atlantis. This event was believed to have occurred about 10,500 years before the birth of Christ. Cayce obtained this information through the famous life readings he performed while he was in a deep trance state.

Other individuals, such as Donnelly, made similar claims. Donnelly described how Atlantean culture and knowledge developed in South America. If we look at the advanced civilization that flourished in Egypt and in South America, it is not hard to imagine this possibility. Astronomy, mathematics, and engineering were highly developed in these parts of the world. Similar architecture in those regions gives some credence to such beliefs.

The people of Atlantis brought the spiritual teachings of the Atlantean Mystery Schools and healing centers to these places. As descendants of the Atlanteans, the aboriginals of the Americas, have a long-established spiritual tradition that is in harmony with the earth. For instance, Tecumseh, the great leader of the Shawnees, was a member of a sacred society loosely based on the Atlantean religion.

Ancient mystery schools were set up in Egypt, and there they flourished. The Egyptian civilization developed its culture and its religion partly from the schools of Atlantis. The ancient Egyptian priesthood became all-powerful in later years, creating a system where the pharaohs depended on the influence of the priesthood to attain and keep their throne.

These schools and healing temples taught many gifted individuals who became masters in their respective fields. The earliest known healer involved in this educational system was Imhotep, a physician-priest of the Third Dynasty (around 2890 B.C.E.); he was the Grand Vizier, architect, scribe, sage, and master healer at the court of the pharaoh Zoser.

Because of his noted ability to heal and his knowledge on herbalism, Imhotep eventually became deified as a god about 525 B.C.E., over 2,300 years after his death. His Egyptian name, Imhotep, became associated with the Greek physician Asklepios during the Greco-Roman era and ultimately, Asklepios became a Greek god in his own right. The Romans adopted Asklepios as they did many other Greek gods. Asklepios, the Greek god of healing, became Romanized as Aesculapius, a son of Apollo, who was himself a major god in the Roman pantheon. The symbol of serpents wrapped about a rod known as the "caduceus," which represented Asklepios in his role as the Greek god of healing, eventually became the symbol of the modern medical profession. All you have to do is spot any ambulance and you will see the caduceus symbol of Asklepios.

# The School at the Sphinx

The ancient schools were deeply entrenched in sacred rituals and secret ceremonies. Most of these ceremonies took place at midnight. Two special sites for these mysterious rituals were by the Sacred Lake at Karnak and in the area surrounding the Sphinx near modern-day Cairo.

The sacred site at the Sphinx predates the one at the Sacred Lake by several thousand years. While the Sacred Lake was a manmade body of water created as a part of the Karnak temple complexes, the great Sphinx is much older than archaeologists estimate (as we will see, new evidence indicates that it is at least 12,000 years old). Below this well-known structure is a complex system of chambers, tunnels, and rooms. In his book, *The Symbolic Prophecy of the Great Pyramid*, H. Spencer Lewis, a late imperator of the Mystical Order of Rosicrucians, describes these chambers below the Sphinx and Great Pyramid in detail. His book, originally published in 1936, presents an illustration of the chambers. In recent times, an extensive examination by archaeologists under the direction of the Egyptian Department of Antiquities has used ultrasound technology to reveal existing tunnels under the sands near the Sphinx.

Supplicants wishing admission to the Egyptian mystery schools gathered before the paws of the Sphinx where fires burned upon an altar. A priest performed the initial ceremony here under the midnight skies, letting the fires of the altar burn bright, entrancing the new initiates into altered states of consciousness. The priest then led the group single file through a large doorway below the breast of the colossal Sphinx. All the supplicants saw an Egyptian winged disc decorating the archway above the entrance door as they

**View of the Sphinx on the Giza Plateau, Egypt.**

descended down a long flight of steps. This entrance, between the "paws" of the Sphinx (see above), was later sealed by the famous Thothmes tablet, which obscured the older winged disc.

At the bottom of the steps was a huge reception chamber where the high priest of the mystical order stood waiting. He was dressed in white garments and enrobed in purple. The high priest then led all the supplicants into the interior of the large chamber and bid them form a semicircle around him as he stood in the north end of this room. At this point, the high priest performed an ancient ritual that initiated or "opened up" the crown and third eye chakras of each initiate present (as we will later discuss in more detail, the crown and third eye chakras are located at the top of the head and forehead areas, respectively). Through special vowel intonations or chants and the use of a large crystal, all who participated in the ritual activated their own energy within, starting a psychic and spiritual process that awakened untapped portions of their minds. This First or Great Initiation was an important event for those who were to begin the intense training of the ancient mystery schools as a way to spiritual enlightenment.

During the initiates' training, many more ceremonies took place in the chamber below the great Sphinx. Students progressed through several levels of studies or degrees, where each entry into the next level required an initiation or ceremony. Advanced students were eventually led from these underground hallways into the Great Pyramid—a structure almost as old as the Sphinx—where a special final initiation was conducted. Successful completion of the studies and all initiations allowed the students to become mystics, physicians, and priests. They were now ready to work in their respective fields.

At the northern part of the reception chamber stood the entrance into a long hallway leading to another, slightly smaller chamber. There were three hallways that led from this smaller chamber: one went due north, directly under the Great Pyramid—it was connected to a secret tunnel that led inside the ancient monument itself; the second hallway headed in a northwesterly direction, to the location of an ancient site; the third hallway went directly south and ended underneath a temple that was used for worship and healing—a hidden set of stairs led down from this temple to the tunnel below.

The second tunnel was of great significance, for it led ultimately to the Atlantean Hall of Records. In this place a huge repository of Atlantean knowledge was stored, arranged in much the same way as a library. Multicolored crystals were kept here and used for the structure's lighting and power. This special place was maintained for centuries by elite members of the Egyptian mystery schools, but was eventually lost or forgotten by later civilizations. In the not too distant future, the Hall of Records will be discovered again.

Today, there is a controversy over the real age of the Sphinx and the Great Pyramid. Certain revelations regarding this controversial subject have recently come to light. Some geologists believe the Sphinx was built in a period predating what we call the ancient Egyptian civilization; they believe the Sphinx was constructed roughly 12,000 years ago. With the help of science, mankind may one day unravel more secrets of the ancient peoples who inspired and built these structures.

Eventually, the ancient mystery schools spread throughout the world. Tibet, India, Greece, Israel, and Persia provide us with some prominent, though widely dispersed examples. In the Americas, similar systems were adopted, such as have been found in the Mayan and Aztec centers. While many believe these similar traditions grew independent of one another, this "mystery" can easily be solved if we consider that the mystery schools all come from a single source: Atlantis. The following sketches of some of the most important mystery schools will show how they evolved throughout the world.

## The Lost Teachings of Jesus

One of the first places influenced by the ancient schools was Heliopolis, a city in the land of Goshen, as it is known in the Bible. This great center of learning was three square miles of area. According to E. A. Wallis Budge, keeper of

Assyrian and Egyptian Antiquities in the British Museum during the early twentieth century, the great learning center is now covered by the waters of the Suez Canal.

Heliopolis was recognized far and wide in the ancient world as a center of teaching, and many gifted persons studied at the prestigious institution there. Jesus of Nazareth (sometimes referred to as Joshua the Galilean) was one of the school's most accomplished students. Jesus was, in fact, an old master who came back to earth to teach and to heal. Many of his "lost years" were spent in Heliopolis learning ancient secrets such as energy healing, divination, human aura interpretation, channeling, or mediumship. He imparted these teachings to the world through his inner circle of twelve disciples and many other students or apostles, including many women. These women worked in particularly prominent positions helping others.

Several modern mystics have uncovered the lost history and teachings of Jesus and his followers. One of the most famous was Edgar Cayce who, while in deep trance, provided detailed information about the life of Jesus Christ in his "life readings." In his book, *The Mystical Life of Jesus,* H. Spencer Lewis describes the "lost years" of Jesus, his mystical education, and the number of people who became his disciples.

Following Jesus' time on earth, Christianity began to change from a balanced system into a patriarchy. Many of the original teachings of Jesus were lost in this time, as mysticism was excised from the practices of the Christian Church. Power, control, and politics became part of the new religion. The mystical teachings of Jesus, descended from Atlantis and the school at Heliopolis, were hidden from the masses for millennia.

# The Essenes

At roughly the same time as the life of Jesus, a mysterious religious sect called the Essenes existed in communities throughout ancient Israel. This sect, whose members created the writings which we know as the Dead Sea Scrolls, was loosely affiliated with Heliopolis.

In reality, the Essenes were divided into two separate sects, one being the monastic order at Qumran on the Dead Sea coast, and the other being an order consisting of married couples located in the Galilee district. Many of these people were gifted healers who worked with the universal healing energy; all were secretly trained in the ancient mysteries of the Egyptian mystery schools, including the healing techniques.

Even though these people were considered a sect of Jews, they were critical of the other major factions within the ancient Jewish religion, the Pharisees and the Sadducees. The Essenes believed that these other factions did not understand their covenant with God. Instead, they believed that it was their sacred trust to prepare the way for the "anointed one" or "Teacher of Righteousness," and the coming of a new world order.

Greeks, Romans, and other Jews commented on the unique qualities of the Essene communities. For instance, Philo of Alexandria, a Jewish philosopher of the first century c.e., described the group in a speech (*Quod Omnis Probus Tiber*, quoted in A. Powell Davies' *The Meaning of the Dead Sea Scrolls*):

> They were a sect of Jews, and lived in Syria Palestine, over 4000 in number, and called *Essaei*, because of

their saintliness; for *hosis*—"saintly," is the same word as *Essaeus*.

Jesus (or Joshua) of Galilee originated from a mystical background rooted in the teachings of the Essenes. Also, both Mary and Joseph, his parents, and his cousin, John the Baptist, claimed ties to the sect and their teachings.

Thanks to the discovery of the Dead Sea Scrolls in 1947, much more is known about the Essenes. We now know that they were more widespread than originally thought, and many of their beliefs and teachings eventually found their way into the New Testament. G. Lankester Harding, the late archaeologist and Director of the Jordanian Department of Antiquities, comments on the significance of the Scrolls (quoted in *The Secret Doctrines of Jesus*, H. Spencer Lewis):

> Most startling disclosure of the Essene documents so far published is that the sect possessed, years before Christ, a terminology and practice that has always been considered uniquely Christian. The Essenes practiced baptism and shared a liturgical repast of bread and wine presided over by a priest. They believed in redemption and the immortality of the soul. Their most important leader was a mysterious figure called the Teacher of Righteousness, a messianic prophet-priest blessed with divine revelation, persecuted and perhaps eventually martyred.

## The Jewish Kabala

The Essenes, though not an integral sect within the Jewish religion, lived in peaceful coexistence with other groups of Jews. In general, the Jewish religion dictates a ritual consciousness in even the most basic and mundane of life's actions. This means that observant Jews at the time of the Essenes and Jesus would have lived with their spirituality as a daily religious influence, inspiration, and companion.

Because the practice of Judaism affected every aspect of life, the mystical realm was seen as the highest point from which a person could commune with the God source. All forms of Judaism can be said to hold mystical beliefs describing how to attain this mystical awareness. Many ideas related to this come from the written works whose teachings form the Kabala (a word meaning "tradition").

The Kabala is a form of esoteric Jewish mysticism that was influenced by the Gnostics, as well as by Greek philosophy and neo-Platonic studies of the early centuries of the common era. The Kabala's teachings were set down in several ancient and medieval books; two of the most influential of these are the *Zohar* and the *Sepher Yezirah*.

The *Zohar*, or the "Book of Splendor," was written in the thirteenth century, while the *Sepher Yezirah*, a name which means the "Book of Creation," was written sometime between the third and sixth centuries in the common era. The teachings found in these books were originally passed down as an oral tradition, from a single teacher to his student.

This tradition of passing wisdom down by word of mouth holds true with the teachings of the Essenes and many other mystical and spiritual groups.

## Hinduism

The ancient mysteries spread through the East as much as they did in the West. Hinduism is the oldest example of this, having developed over several millennia in India. Today it is one of the world's oldest living religions.

At the center of the religion sits a triad of gods: Brahma the Creator, Vishnu the Preserver, and Shiva the Destroyer. This is the oldest holy trinity on earth (the Father, the Son, and the Holy Ghost of Christianity came later, from the same concept of a "triple divinity").

As a religion roughly 4,000 years old and still "intact," Hinduism provides a way of life as well as an organized religious system for its followers. There are no formal decrees or strict religious doctrines in Hinduism; rather, worshippers can choose deities who best suit their mortal hopes and needs.

As Hinduism developed, the study of the release of energy through the human body also became a prime focus of the religion. This release of sexual energy, known as Kundalini or "serpent power," was accomplished through the sexual union of a man and a woman. The path to spiritual enlightenment lay in the release of this powerful force through the chakras or energy centers of both partners. Sexual union led to cosmic or divine union as discussed in the Kama Sutra, the ancient Hindu text dealing with this amazing energy.

## Buddha

Following the birth of Hinduism in India, another example of the ancient teachings came to that region in the form of Buddhism. The teachings of Buddha established a firm hold in Tibet and northern India, with the doctrine of reincarnation forming the centerpiece for the religion. Buddha, an enlightened master like Jesus, taught the ancient mysteries to many of his followers.

Gautama Buddha is believed to have been born in Nepal around 563 B.C.E. Born a prince in Nepal, he was originally known as Siddhartha Gautama. Later, he was given the title of respect "Buddha," which means "Enlightened One."

Prince Gautama lived in wealth and luxury for many years. One day while travelling through a part of his domain, he observed the devastating poverty his subjects suffered. After this time, he denounced his nobility and became a seeker of wisdom.

At first, Gautama studied the ancient sacred writings of India, the Vedas and the Upanishads, which are the core texts of the Hindu religion. The Upanishads (composed circa 800 B.C.E.) are more spiritual and philosophical in nature, while the Vedas treat mythological themes. Although they were important, these works did not provide the "answer" Gautama was seeking.

One day, while meditating beneath a bo tree, Gautama suddenly received divine inspiration. In a flash of realization, he became Buddha. As the Enlightened One, he developed Buddhism, a new religion based on his profound personal experience mixed with the wisdom he had learned while studying the ancient teachings of Hinduism.

## Persia

Another region that embraced the wisdom of the ancient teachings was Persia (modern Iran). About 2,600 years ago, Zoroaster, another master teacher, taught the mysteries to the Persians as the ancient religion of light, known today as Zoroastrianism. This religion spoke of the struggle of light versus darkness and good versus evil. Zoroaster was said to have been born of a virgin, one of many striking similarities between the life story of Jesus Christ and this Persian spiritual teacher.

Zoroaster was probably born in the northern part of the Persian Empire. Legend has it that Ahura Mazda, the god of light and goodness, impregnated a girl with light. From this divine union came Zoroaster's mother. Again like Christ, Zoroaster was also a wise child who conversed in a knowledgeable way with adults.

Then, around the age of thirty, Zoroaster turned to religion. After the god Ahura Mazda purified him, he went into the desert to meditate and seek spiritual enlightenment. There, Zoroaster received his divine inspiration.

From his enlightened state, he gave his teachings in the form of a holy text, the Zend Avesta. These sacred scriptures discuss the belief in one god, omnipotent, who has the power of truth, light, and life. Zoroaster taught his students to have kind hearts and do kind deeds for others. The purity of the human soul was central to his philosophy and spiritual teaching.

Today in India, there is a group called the Parsis who still follow Zoroaster's ancient religion of light. Also, descendants of the Persian people still practice the rituals of Zoroaster in Iran and throughout the world.

## Greece

The Greeks adapted the ancient mysteries in several special cult centers. The most famous were the Eleusinian Mysteries, which became popular throughout the Mediterranean world. Eventually, these mysteries gained a foothold in

Roman society. People came by the thousands to Eleusis for initiation into the mysteries. Adherents were involved in secret rituals taking place within sacred sites and temples built around a holy precinct; this was the continuation of ancient mysteries which had come from Atlantis via Egypt. Even Roman emperors were initiated into the Eleusinian Mysteries: Marcus Aurelius, emperor from 161 C.E. until his death in 180, was one of the many initiates.

We derive the word for "mystery" from the Greeks. Their word *mystes* referred to knowledge that was secret, as opposed to the general, nonreligious meaning for which we use the word today; in our modern usage we have lost the religious aspect that was originally at the heart of this word. The ancient Greeks' mysteries or "secret traditions" were a central element of the ancient mystery schools.

Since interest in the mystery schools of Greece was spread across Europe, North Africa, and the Middle East by Roman expansion, many later cultures in those areas ultimately owe their religious character to the Greeks. The traditions they practiced long ago can still be found in many modern rituals.

## The Magi

At the time that Rome was expanding into the Mediterranean world (within the lifetime of Christ), there lived a group of wise men referred to as "Magi" (singular, "Magus"), a word meaning "wise men." Most of the Magi were from Persia, others lived in Babylon and in Egypt. The Magi, who were all disciples of Zoroaster, were highly trained in healing and metaphysical skills. Many rulers throughout the ancient Middle East held them in high esteem.

The Magi were experts in astrology and astronomy: they studied the stars and incorporated their findings into their religious practices. Most people today hear of the Magi in their role as astrologers, since the "three wise men" mentioned in the New Testament account of Jesus' birth were Magi. But few people realize that a number of the ancient mystery schools were expecting the birth of an enlightened master, something that the story of the "three wise men" reflects.

In fact, there was a prophecy among the Magi, the Essenes, members of the Egyptian mystery schools, and others that predicted the return of a spiritual master or Messiah (from Hebrew *moshiach*, "anointed one"). The advent of such a person was a central theme among these groups. For the astrologically tuned Magi, the celestial event, known as the Star of Bethlehem, was a sign that the "anointed one" had in fact returned to earth.

## Mithraism

While the Magi searched the heavens for a sign, Mithraism, a religion originally from India, was gaining in influence throughout the Roman Empire. With strong Persian characteristics, this religion was steeped in sacred rituals and initiations, qualities which the ever-receptive Imperial Roman society found appealing. At the center of the cult was Mithra, the god of light and truth.

As the Christian Church became the dominant religion in the Roman world, it borrowed many of the rituals and traditions of Mithraism in order to convert the masses. The burning of incense such as frankincense and myrrh, the lighting of candles, the sacred rites performed by priests wearing colorful vestments, and baptism by water are all part of the organized Church today. All were borrowed from ancient religious ceremonies devoted to Mithra and his kindred, "pagan" deities.

## Christianity and the Loss of Spirituality

Just as the Roman Empire was reaching its greatest size, stretching from the British Isles to the Persian Gulf region, a religious struggle was born in Palestine that would last for hundreds of years . . . and outlive the Empire by a millennium and a half. From the time of Christ's teaching on earth, Christianity began to gain in popularity and simultaneously eclipse Greco-Roman paganism. At first, many of the Roman emperors who worshiped the Greco-Roman gods persecuted Christians. For example, the emperor Domitian (reigned circa 81 C.E.) outlawed Christianity altogether, punishing those who rejected the Roman gods and rewarded those who turned in "secret Christians."

Persecution of Christians continued until Constantine the Great became emperor in 306 C.E. Known as the "first Christian emperor," he helped Christianity become the dominant religion of the Roman Empire. Within fifty years of his death, all non-Christian faiths had been outlawed throughout the Empire.

Unfortunately, as it became the sole religion practiced over vast sections of Europe, Asia, and Africa, the Christian Church had become a persecutor of other faiths. In Alexandria, the great library was burned by a Christian mob; much of the knowledge contained in the form of countless scrolls and books were lost forever in this purge of pagan literature and thought. In Rome, the bishop of the Christian Church became supreme as a particular sect of the religion won out over other, more tolerant forms. Soon, the Church was a powerful political and religious institute, enshrining politics while ignoring true spirituality. At that time, mainstream Christianity lost its connection to the true teachings of Jesus.

In the first centuries after the triumph of Christianity over Roman paganism, several groups loyal to the true teachings of Jesus met clandestinely and taught their wisdom. The Gnostics, one such sect that followed Jesus' true teachings, challenged the organized Christian Church (the name "Gnostic" is derived from the Greek work *gnosis* which means "knowledge"). They believed in the spiritual teachings of Jesus, and were sometimes even called the "Jesus sect." But, pressured and persecuted by the Church, it eventually went "underground," taking its spiritual wisdom along with it. Gnosticism appeared to have been destroyed.

While it was seeking to snuff out rival faiths and gaining influence throughout Europe, Christianity became internally more conservative, if not repressive, regarding sexuality, mysticism, and personal individuality. By the late 1470s, this repressiveness entered into a very dark era. Anyone practicing mysticism or the ancient mysteries lived in constant fear of the Inquisition, whose agents sought to uncover, punish, and destroy any alternative or dissenting religious views. The Inquisition, best known for its particularly brutal presence in Spain, forced still more individuals and groups "underground," where all studies were conducted in hidden places, totally in secret. The Freemasons and Rosicrucians, as representatives of the Great White

Brotherhood or ancient mystery schools, kept the teachings derived from ancient Atlantis and Egypt alive through mysterious and discreet ways.

Other groups that came up against the early Christian Church were the Celts and the Druids, representing a hugely diverse group of related cultures all espousing an intense spirituality and closeness to the earth. The Celtic religion was based on a reverence for Mother Earth, a being viewed as the nurturer, protector, and provider for her people; many Celtic rituals were performed based on the cycles of the sun and moon. This was not to last, for as the Celtic peoples converted to Christianity, they forgot their native culture and its traditions, opening the door for Christianity to prevail in the British Isles and parts of central  and northern Europe. Other "pagan religions," such as those found in Scandinavia and agricultural communities of Europe, were also lost in this shift in religious ideologies.

Finally, in the Americas, as Europeans explored and settled the land, the Native Americans were conquered and assimilated into European ways. The spiritual way of life of these original inhabitants was nearly destroyed, as their lands and natural resources were robbed from them. The greed and materialism of Europe took precedence over the spiritualism of the Americas, spiritualism which could also claim its roots in the teachings of ancient Atlantis.

## Conclusion

Although it would appear that the true teachings of the ancient masters have been lost, or at least buried "underground," new discoveries reveal that the truth cannot be suppressed forever. For example, in 1945, archaeologists found a series of Gnostic writings or "gospels" at Nag Hammadi in Egypt. Some of these writings are reportedly the preserved words of Jesus Christ; among these texts was found a work which scholars refer to as the "Gospel of Thomas," a fifth gospel.

Now, as we enter into a new millennium, the hope remains that we will reverse the negative trend of the previous millennia and enter a world where spirituality reigns supreme once again. The following pages will discuss the original, true teachings of Jesus Christ, the original studies of Atlantean and Egyptian mystery schools, and the secret techniques needed to develop psychic and spiritual attributes.

# Chapter 2

## *The Third Eye Chakra*

Grown men may learn from little children for
the hearts of little children are pure and therefore, the Great Spirit may show to them many
things which other people miss.
—Black Elk (Native American
Spiritual Leader, 1863–1950)

The ancients believed in the duality of the universe. In their
cosmology, there was the macrocosm as reflected in the
heavens and the stars, and the microcosm as reflected in
the earth and in nature. They also believed that this duality
existed in human beings: we possess both a physical body
and a psychic body. The difference between the two was
that the psychic body was contained within the physical
body, but it manifested at a much higher vibration than its
physical "shell." Accordingly, along with physical organs
there were in fact psychic organs residing within the
human form.

## The Aura and Chakras

Everything in nature is surrounded by energy patterns.
Trees, plants, and animals all possess energy patterns or
radiations of multicolored lights. Humans are no excep-

tion. An amazing energy field surrounds the human body; this is often referred to as the "aura," the electromagnetic field, or the human energy field.

Within the aura are energy centers called "chakras." In Sanskrit, the word chakra literally means "wheel of light." There are seven major chakras and about 120 minor chakras contained within the human aura. All of these chakras are indirectly connected to certain parts of the physical body by way of the aura and psychic body. These centers are located above and around areas of the body and exist at a very high frequency or rate of vibration.

The primary chakras are also indirectly linked to the seven major glands of the endocrine system by way of the sympathetic nervous division and the central nervous system. These chakras are located up and down the body, from the head to the reproductive organs. Both the sympathetic and central nervous systems receive energy or vibrations from the seven major chakras and direct it into seven major glands in the human body. Meanwhile, the vibrations are also sent to other organs and areas within the physical body. Keep in mind that everything in nature has different rates of vibrations. The chakra system will be discussed in more detail later.

## The Third Eye and the Pineal Gland

In this chapter, you will learn ancient techniques to awaken or, more accurately, *re*awaken the "third eye," one of the primary energy centers in the psychic body. Once this is accomplished, you will be on a path towards psychic development and spiritual growth.

When the term "third eye" is used, it refers to the sixth chakra or third eye chakra, located in the center of the forehead. It is closely associated with the pineal gland. Lying inside the brain, this particular gland remains mysterious to medical science. Nevertheless, scientists agree that the pineal gland functions as an internal clock in some way, and that it is affected indirectly by light. As darkness approaches, it activates the release of a hormone called melatonin; when daylight arrives, the secretion of this hormone ceases. Many scientists also believe that seasonal mood swings (such as "SAD," seasonal affective disorder) can be attributed to this gland. In the last few years, doctors and researchers have shown that light therapy can be an effective treatment for patients suffering from seasonal mood disorders.

The pineal gland is actually a part of the endocrine glandular system of the body. The term endocrine comes from the Greek words *endo*, which means "inside" or "within," and *krinein*, which means "to separate." These endocrine glands, sometimes referred to as "ductless glands," release certain hormones directly into the bloodstream of the body. All the glands of the endocrine system work in harmony with one another.

The pineal gland is also believed to be associated with reproduction and works in conjunction with the pituitary gland as well as the hypothalamus region of the brain. The pineal gland has been misnamed; it is actually an organ.

The French philosopher, Rene Descartes, thought that the pineal gland was the "seat of the soul" where mind and body met. In ancient times, mystics and students on the

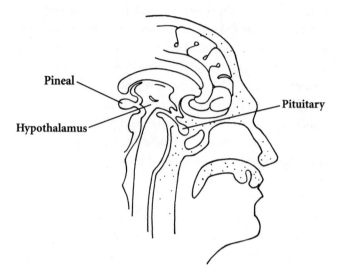

Pineal

Pituitary

Hypothalamus

**This diagram shows the location of the pineal and pituitary glands, as well as the hypothalamus region.**

spiritual path were aware of this mind-body connection. In fact, the proper development and use of this gland was the key to intuition and psychic attributes. It is here that the intuitive ability and creativity is stored.

As children, our pineal glands function properly, allowing us to use our intuition, creativity, and psychic abilities freely. There are many children who can see auras or lights around people and others who can see and communicate with deceased relatives, spirit guides, and angels. This is the source of many children's "imaginary friends."

Usually around the age of twelve, many children start to lose some of their psychic abilities, not because of puberty but because our society discourages their use. Our educational system emphasizes logical thinking and analysis. Many parents, educators, authority figures, and other adults discourage children from using their psychic abilities by dismissing it as imaginative or accusing the child of making up stories. For example, an uncle or an aunt might dismiss the "imaginary friend" as pure imagination. Perhaps a grade-school teacher admonishes the child for talking about the colors he can see around everybody. This closed-minded attitude caused irreparable damage to many young gifted children. Under these conditions, the pineal gland becomes atrophied and begins to calcify as less energy is directed there. This major physical change in the pineal causes a loss of intuitive and psychic abilities. By age twenty, many young adults are completely unable to use these abilities.

Fortunately, our society is becoming more open-minded and tolerant towards imaginative children. Many adults are now encouraging children to express their creativity and explore their psychic gifts. This more enlightened attitude helps to keep the pineal gland activated and the third eye chakra functioning well. The third eye chakra, which is directly affected by the activated pineal gland, will in turn activate or "open up" and allow these children of light to shine forth in a spiritually evolving world. The rising awareness or consciousness mentioned in chapter 1 refers in part to the opening of the third eye chakra. These young people will bring many of their attributes through into adulthood to help our awakening society.

Adults too are now experiencing activation of their pineal glands, a state leading ultimately to their third eye

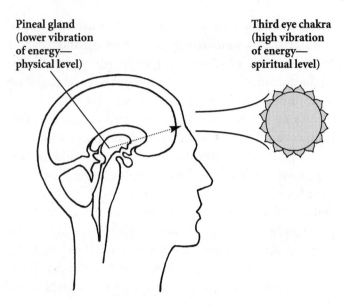

Pineal gland
(lower vibration
of energy—
physical level)

Third eye chakra
(high vibration
of energy—
spiritual level)

**Illustration of the third eye chakra and its connection with the pineal gland.**

chakra opening. As this phenomenon occurs, these individuals go through emotional and physical states. Some feel an intense urge or desire to work in a more altruistic field that will benefit the world at large. Whatever their feelings, though, all experience a drive to learn more, especially in the realms of alternative healing and psychic exploration. Earning money and achieving affluence takes second place to serving others and making a difference in the world. Their daily existence, which before consisted of mundane employment, collecting material things and close-minded attitudes, is changing dramatically. As they achieve higher consciousness, they notice that something is missing in their lives. Soon, just paying the bills, working, watching television, and existing within a nine-to-five mentality seem less important. These people start to believe that there must be more to life. As they *awaken*, they search for answers about the meaning of life and their reason for living. In their search for a life mission, they are taking the first steps on a spiritual path.

On a physical level, many of these newly awakened adults start to feel pressure, strange sensations, or even headaches in the forehead and temple areas. If he or she does not know what is happening, a person may attribute these physical sensations to stress or illness. These sensations in the forehead and temple areas may be followed by pressure or tingling sensations on the top of the head and all over the head. These sensations indicate that the pineal gland has been activated and that the third eye chakra is opening. These newly awakened adults are actually returning to their true self and to their intuitive and creative ways, the ways of little children who are naturally blessed with these gifts.

Consider the following analogy for a moment. Psychically, the pineal gland (which is shaped like a pine cone) can be compared to a single grape on a vine. The sun's warmth and the rain allow the grape to be healthy and full-sized. With time, however, this grape dries up, becomes withered. In simple terms, it becomes a raisin. In children, the pineal gland is healthy, active, and full-sized. This state continues in a person until around age twelve to fourteen. When a person reaches full adulthood, the pineal gland is almost dried up, much like a raisin, and it is atrophied. When this occurs, a person loses all or most of his or her intuitive abilities even though the pineal gland still performs its function on a physical level. To regain these lost abilities, this gland must be reactivated. The key to accomplishing this is to have energy sent to this area. Then the raisin becomes a grape once more and the pineal functions as it once did in childhood.

In 1956, a book entitled *The Third Eye* was published in England. Written by T. Lobsang Rampa, who claimed to be a Tibetan medical lama gifted with esoteric knowledge, the book describes an unusual and dangerous operation performed on the author by monks. According to Rampa, these men heated a stick in a fire and then carefully inserted it into his pineal gland. This procedure then activated Rampa's pineal gland and awakened all of his psychic potential. The pressure and vibration created by the stick's insertion are suppose to have triggered a reaction within the gland. Even though this is a crude and dangerous way to initiate the awakening process, it does show that the Tibetans had an understanding of the importance of the pineal gland and the third eye.

Fortunately, there is an easier and safer method to awaken these important psychic organs.

## The Third Eye Technique

An ancient technique has been preserved for reactivating the pineal gland, a secret exercise passed down through the centuries. The concept behind this technique is to create a vibration within the head, specifically within the pineal gland and area surrounding it.

What is the source of such a vibration? It is derived from power of words produced by the human voice. The proper tone induced by a voice can create an energy or vibration that profoundly affects a human brain. The method is sometimes referred to as toning, chanting, or "doing vibrational work."

By chanting a specific sound based on a certain musical note, a vibration or sound movement can be triggered within the pineal. If this exercise is done properly, it will have the same results as the procedure performed by the Tibetan monks on Lobsang Rampa.

The intonation or chant to use is THOH. THOH rhymes with "toe" and is pronounced just as it appears. It is chanted in one syllable using a mid to high C musical note. If you are not musically inclined, do not worry about attaining the exact frequency; an approximation is just as effective. Just remember that the proper sound is an alto note, midrange between a deep bass note and a high tenor note. In other words, to attain the right vibration, you simply chant THOH, not in a deep low voice and not in a high voice, but in a voice between both of these ranges.

To begin the exercise, take in a deep breath through your nose and hold it as long as is comfortable, then slowly release it through slightly parted lips. Repeat this twice more. This breathing exercise allows you to pull in vital life energy or Universal Energy into your lungs and then into your whole body. It also slows down your brain wave patterns from a beta level or waking state to a light alpha level, an altered state of consciousness. The alpha brain wave pattern is the state where meditation begins. You become more relaxed, making it easier to concentrate on the intonation of THOH.

Next, take another deep breath through your nose and hold it for a few seconds. Just before you release your breath through your mouth, place your tongue through slightly parted teeth. Put a light pressure onto the tongue with your teeth. This is the same process as saying the "th" part of "the." Once your tongue is in this position, release your breath slowly through your mouth saying T-h-h-o-h-h until all of your air has been expelled. Your should feel the air moving past your tongue and teeth. If this technique is done properly, you will also experience a pressure or sensation in your jaw and cheeks.

Repeat this technique twice with a few moments rest between each vowel chant. The Thoh chant should be said three times in succession in the first attempt. About twenty-four hours later, repeat the chanting technique in the same manner, saying Thoh three times with a slight interval in between each chant.

This exercise should be done one more time, about twenty-four hours after the second try. This third day of saying the vowel chant Thoh should be the final time. This is a one-time technique that does not have to be performed over and over like most exercises. If you wish to experiment with this vowel chant again, wait at least two weeks before attempting it again.

This Third Eye Exercise creates a vibration or pressure on your jaw and face, causing this vibration or energy to work its way into the pineal gland. This vibrational energy triggers a resonating effect upon the pineal and activates it. Keep in mind that Thoh should be said or almost sung in a strong voice using a mid-C musical note. An approximate midrange sound is sufficient.

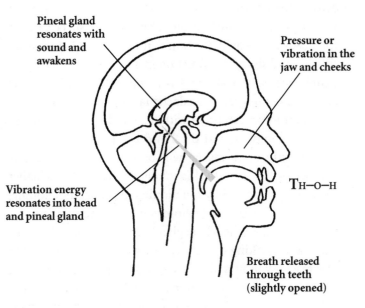

Pineal gland resonates with sound and awakens

Pressure or vibration in the jaw and cheeks

Vibration energy resonates into head and pineal gland

Tн–о–н

Breath released through teeth (slightly opened)

**This illustration shows the position of the tongue and teeth while performing the Third Eye Exercise.**

For some of you, this ancient technique that has been passed down through the centuries may not seem to have any effect at first. Do not worry as the effects of this exercise can be very subtle. You may have many physical and psychic experiences within a short period of time, or such experiences may not manifest for several weeks.

## Physical Effects Resulting from the Third Eye Technique

One of the first experiences that you may have is a headache or pressure in the center of the forehead, just above the brow. This sensation may feel like it is originating from within, usually an inch or more beneath the surface of the forehead. This is an indication that the pineal gland is reactivating and starting to function in a healthy manner. Some people, whose pineal gland is completely atrophied, may experience a migraine headache lasting for several hours. This discomfort can occur within a few days or a few weeks after the completion of the Third Eye Exercise. For most, the pressure or headache will be considerably less. The severity of the side effect is totally dependent on whether the pineal gland is fully functioning, partially functioning, or completely atrophied before you begin the exercises.

In most cases, the pineal gland is already somewhat activated and working effectively, at least to some degree. For this reason you may simply feel a pressure or sensation in the forehead; the sensation may even be pleasing to some.

If you do not feel anything at all, you may try the experiment again in about three weeks. This is necessary only in rare circumstances. Sometimes an individual will feel little or no physical sensations from this special exercise, but he or she will start to experience certain psychic phenomena. This is a sign that the exercise has been successful and the awakening process has begun.

After the occurrence of headache or pressure in the forehead, you may wake up one morning feeling a throbbing or tingling sensation in your forehead; it may feel like a goose bump. When this happens, the feeling may be so intense that you will look into a mirror to see what is there, but there will be nothing to see. Your forehead will look as it should. However, the strange sensation of pulsing or throbbing will continue through most of the day. This is the final physiological event that you will experience after the Third Eye Exercise. It indicates that your pineal gland is once more fully awakened, activated, and functioning as it did when you were a child. As your pineal gland activates and balances itself, the rest of your endocrine glandular system will become more balanced and operate more harmoniously.

Eventually, this strange sensation will stop. You may find yourself becoming lightheaded on occasion and start daydreaming more. For those of you who already do a lot of daydreaming or drifting, this change of awareness may not be noticed as much. The daydreaming and lightheadedness means that your brainwave patterns are changing, slowing down. Instead of functioning and working in a normal waking state (i.e., using a beta brainwave pattern during the day), you are starting to operate in an alpha brainwave pattern or, more accurately, a light trance state. This state of consciousness is the state you should be in during most of your day. A person works more effectively, can handle more stress, and finds that time flows more quickly while in this altered state.

Eventually, you will find a balance between the beta state and the alpha state and daydream less often. You will start to function normally in a light alpha level. To outside observers, you will appear fully awake. No one will notice that you are now working and living your life in an altered state of consciousness.

Incidentally, you can learn more quickly and memorize facts and dates more easily when in this relaxed state, because you are using more of your brain's immense capacity.

## Psychic Effects Resulting from the Third Eye Technique

The third eye chakra or energy center starts to activate and "open up" once the pineal gland has been activated.

On a psychic level, the results are as follows:

- Intuitive abilities increase
- Creativity expands
- Clairvoyant gifts develop
- Empathic abilities increase
- Ability to see and sense human auras obtained
- Clairaudient gifts develop

These gifts and abilities will start to unfold as your third eye opens. The Third Eye Technique is a powerful and effective way to develop your psychic abilities. Instead of struggling with life and striving to reach your true human potential over years, you will begin to raise your consciousness and start using your gifts easily. This will occur in a short period of time usually over a six-week to one-year period.

The Third Eye Technique is the key to increased psychic development and spiritual enlightenment. With the awakening of your pineal gland and your third eye chakra, you will step onto your path, pointed in your life's true direction.

# Chapter 3

# *The Crown Chakra*

Eternal wisdom, scatter the darkness of our
ignorance.
—Archbishop Alcuin (735-804 c.e.)

The Ancient Mystery Schools possessed certain techniques
to guide students and seekers onto the path of psychic
development and spiritual enlightenment. Thousands of
years ago, during the "Great Initiation Rite" performed in a
chamber below the Great Sphinx, the high priest uttered
special sounds to awaken the initiates' psychic selves. Thoh,
the chant to stimulate the pineal gland and awaken the
third eye chakra, was the first vibrational chant the high
priest employed.

Following this, he would intone a second chant. This
was designed to stimulate the pituitary gland residing deep
within the heads of the initiates. This gland is directly
linked to the crown chakra (also known as the first chakra)
and its higher vibrational frequencies. The crown chakra is
located on top of the head.

Before performing the second chant, it is important to
understand a little about both the pituitary gland and the
crown chakra.

The pituitary gland is located in the center of the human
head. If you look at the bridge of a person's nose and then

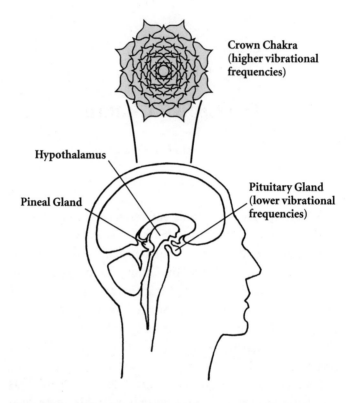

Crown Chakra
(higher vibrational
frequencies)

Hypothalamus

Pineal Gland

Pituitary Gland
(lower vibrational
frequencies)

**Illustration of the pituitary gland inside the brain and the location of the crown chakra.**

imagine a straight line going about three inches further into the head, the gland lies at that point directly on the line. It is about the size of a pea. Even though it is often called the master gland, it is subservient to the hypothalamus region of the brain and can be considered an appendage attached to the base of this area of the brain.

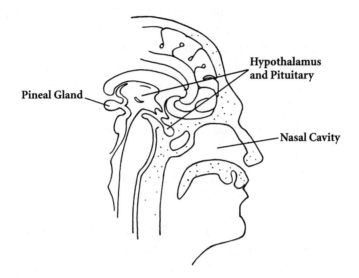

**Illustration showing the location of the pituitary gland, hypothalamus, and pineal gland in relation to the nasal cavity.**

The pituitary is actually divided into two portions. The front portion is referred to as the "anterior pituitary," while the back is called the "posterior pituitary." Both portions have distinct but complementary functions within the body. The anterior pituitary is responsible for the release of a growth hormone called somatotropin. This hormonal secretion controls the development of bones, muscles, and other organs. The anterior portion also exerts direct influence on many of the other endocrine glands. For example, the anterior pituitary affects the thyroid through the release of a thyroid-stimulating hormone called thyrotropic. The posterior pituitary affects the smooth muscle system.

Modern medicine understands only the physical aspects of this gland. It ignores the importance of the pituitary gland as a mystical key to spiritual enlightenment and psychic unfolding. Throughout human history, some individuals believed that science and spirituality could complement each other and work together.

> Science and Metaphysics would come nearer together, would in fact work absolutely hand in hand.
> —William James (philosopher and scientist, 1842-1910)

Hopefully, more individuals will understand the relationship between the physical and the spiritual in the near future. From this heightened understanding, we can create a more spiritual world.

The pituitary gland is closely associated with the crown chakra energy center. Extremely high psychic and spiritual energies vibrate within and above this chakra. This is a form of the Universal Energy which permeates everything in creation: it can be found in the air, in the water, in the trees, plants, and in the earth itself. Normally, this cosmic essence cannot be seen because of its high rate of vibration but it can be felt and experienced by individuals trained and evolved enough to sense its presence.

Everyone experiences the existence of television and radio waves, though they cannot be seen. By turning on a radio or a television receiver, we can "experience" these waves, which are vibrating at a high rate. A rate of vibration is a frequency and can be measured by the number of vibrations per second or cycles per second (CPS).

Keep in mind that everything vibrates at a certain frequency. A common rock in the ground vibrates at a lower rate than a living animal. The human body and all its organs, glands, nerves, and tissues vibrate at a much higher frequency than an inert rock. Each cell, organ, tissue, and physical portion of the body has its own special frequency or cycles per second. Illness or disease occurs when one organ or area of the human body is out of sync or harmony with the other parts of the body.

With all this in mind, we can again consider the crown chakra. If you can think of this energy center as the receiver tuning in to the high cosmic Universal Energy, as well as psychic energy, you will have a basic understanding of some of the secret principles that were taught in the ancient mystery schools of Atlantis and Egypt.

The Universal Energy enters into the human aura by way of the crown chakra and through the top of the head. As it enters into the human brain, it starts to slow its rate of vibration. The pineal gland, if functioning properly, serves as a special type of transformer that receives the cosmic energy and transforms it to a lower frequency. The energy then moves through the hypothalamus region of the brain into the pituitary gland. At this stage, the pituitary gland works as a special transformer that lowers or steps down the cosmic and psychic energy to an even lower frequency. From this point, the energy is released into other parts of the brain where it becomes assimilated and recognizable as any of a number of psychic phenomena, healing energy, intuition, divine inspiration, communication with the higher self, or the inner voice. Abilities and psychic gifts experienced in this manner include:

- Clairaudient abilities: psychically hearing voices and sounds
- Clairvoyant abilities: psychically seeing visions and events
- Clairsentient gifts: psychically feeling or sensing emotions

In metaphysics, the pineal and pituitary glands may be thought of as similar in purpose to step-down transformers in electronics, transformers that alter, lower, or change the frequency or type of electrical currents. They transform one type of energy to another form.

Both the pineal and the pituitary must be operating fully and in a healthy manner in order for this process of energy transformation to take place. The crown and third eye energy centers must also be properly activated and "opened."

The Third Eye Exercise explained in chapter 2 was the first step necessary to help facilitate this process. The vibration created in the pineal gland activates or awakens this area of the brain. It also sends a vibration through the hypothalamus into the pituitary gland. This in turn affects and helps activate the pituitary.

About seven to ten days after completion of the Thoh chant exercise, you will be ready to move on to the second exercise. The intervening period will have allowed the Third Eye Exercise to activate the pineal gland and to stimulate the pituitary gland.

# Universal Energy Spectrum Phenomena

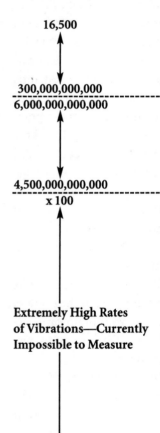

| Frequency (CPS or Hz) | Manifestations of Spectrum |
|---|---|
| 16,500 ↕ 300,000,000,000 | **Electrical Spectrum** *Includes radio, television, microwaves, infrared, heat* |
| 6,000,000,000,000 ↕ 4,500,000,000,000 | **Normal Human Vision Spectrum** *Includes colors, physical manifestations* |
| x 100 ↕ | **Extended Human Vision Spectrum Used by Psychically Gifted Persons** *Includes seeing auras and chakras spirit guides and angels, healing, and spiritual energy* |
| **Extremely High Rates of Vibrations—Currently Impossible to Measure** ↕ | **Universal, Psychic, and Spiritual Energy Spectrum** *Includes psychic phenomena, human aura field, chakra energy centers, healing energy, astral levels, soul manifestation, psychic abilities* |

Chart showing the Universal Energy spectrum and how all manifestations are based on rates of vibration. Notice that the Universal, psychic, and spiritual energies vibrate at various frequencies which cannot be measured by today's scientific standards.

## The Crown Chakra Exercise

As mentioned above, this exercise is the second special chant performed by the Egyptian high priest during the "Great Initiation Rite." Not only was this ritual conducted in a secret chamber below the Sphinx, but also at the Sacred Lake at Karnak years later. This arcane ritual, practiced with both chants, many candles, strong incense, and sacred invocations was the ceremony originally performed in Atlantis and later adopted by the Egyptian mystery institutions; both Mithraism and Christianity adopted some of these practices. The sound or chant that you will be using is MAY, pronounced just like the month of May. This particular sound can be expressed in a mid-C musical note or a midrange between bass and tenor. Once again, the chant does not have to be exactly on key. An approximation is fine. You simply use the musical note that works best for you.

Begin by taking three or four deep, relaxing breaths. Feel your breath going in and out of your lungs. When exhaling, allow your breath to leave slowly and steadily each time. This type of breathing will slow down your heart rate, blood pressure and, most importantly, your brainwave patterns. This relaxed state will make it easier for you to perform the exercise in an effective manner.

Now, return to normal breathing and start to focus all your concentration on your forehead just above the bridge of the nose. Your concentration should be about one inch above the eyebrow level and in the middle of the forehead. Keep concentrating on this point above the nose for a few minutes until you start to feel pressure, warmth, or some type of sensation in this area. If you do not feel any sensations after a few moments, don't worry about it.

Continue focusing on this area which is the third eye energy center.

Once you have concentrated for a little while, take a deep breath in, hold it for about five seconds, then chant the word M-A-Y through your mouth as you expel all your breath in a long, slow manner. As you are singing or chanting this sound, feel the energy or vibration going into your head, first through the third eye area of the forehead, then inside to the middle of the brain . . . and even to the top of your head where the crown chakra is located.

Once you have expelled all your breath, return to normal breathing once more. Take a few seconds to relax.

After this brief respite, repeat the process. Do the deep breathing, the MAY chant, and the slow, gradual release of breath in the same way you did it the first time. Remember to concentrate on your forehead (third eye chakra area), then the middle of your brain, and finally the top of your head (crown chakra area). Allow the vibration of M-A-Y to work through your head. The MAY chant can be done a third time if desired.

The Crown Chakra Exercise may be performed whenever you feel the need to use it. Feel free to make the exercise a part of your weekly spiritual regimen throughout your life.

Once you have tried this exercise, just return to your normal business. The vibrational energy will start to work within your brain even if at first you are not aware of any unusual feelings.

## Effects of the Crown Chakra Exercise

For some, the effects of the chant will be quite noticeable during and shortly after completing the exercise. For others it will appear as a gradual effect.

Some of the effects experienced from the Third Eye Exercise in chapter 2 will also occur during the Crown Chakra Exercise. There will be some changes in many of these effects as described in chapter 2, as well as new experiences, resulting in the awakening of certain psychic gifts.

The headaches or unusual pressures (commonly called "third eye headache") associated with the Тнон chant will decrease or disappear and be replaced with energy sensations or rushes through parts of the head. You may feel energy inside your head as the vibrations of the May chant continue to work on the pituitary gland, hypothalamus, and pineal gland. Sensations will start on the top of the head, the sides, and even into the back of the head. These feelings are referred to as "tingles," simply because the energy feels like tingling sensations moving over parts of the scalp. It is a very peaceful, gentle experience for most people. This is a major indication that the pituitary gland has been stimulated on a physical level and has activated the crown chakra to open up on a psychic level. When the crown chakra becomes fully awakened, the result is a sensation of energy or "tingles" completely covering the head right down to the ears. This may feel like a physical crown being set on top of the skull, hence the name of this chakra.

The headaches or pressures felt after the Third Eye Exercise of chapter 2 will lessen and eventually disappear as the vibration from the May chant starts to work inside your head. There will be some feelings of lightheadedness for a while as your brainwaves slow down from the waking or beta state to the alpha state or light trance condition. This is normal; in fact, this is the desired effect. The "spacy" or lightheaded sensation will end in a short time and a heightened sense of awareness will remain. Your body and brain are changing and adapting to the vibrations of  higher energy, resulting in your ability to operate efficiently in an alpha state while fully awake. Individuals attaining this ability are more effective, healthier, happier, and less stressed in life.

If performed properly, the MAY chant will activate your pituitary gland, balancing it and assisting in balancing the rest of the endocrine glandular system. Among other benefits, this causes a major slowdown of the aging process!

If the Crown Chakra Exercise is performed in the evening, some positive results may be seen the next morning. Gaze at your face in the mirror immediately upon rising. You may notice that your face and your skin look smoother and younger. Your eyes may look clearer and brighter.

Another benefit derived from this vibrational work is a sense of well-being or, in some cases, a mild sense of euphoria. The vibrational energy placed upon the pituitary and surrounding area, as well as focusing on this area of the brain results in the release of endorphins into the bloodstream; these will give you a "high" much like a "runner's high." For individuals suffering from mood swings or depression, the Crown Chakra Exercise can alleviate the problem and help to create a balanced emotional state within; the M-A-Y vibrational work has helped many people suffering from manic depression.

## Psychic Effects

Once the pituitary gland has been properly activated on the physical level, the crown chakra will also be activated on a psychic level. With this activation or "opening up" of the crown chakra, more psychic gifts will unfold. They include:

- Intuitive abilities increase
- Creativity expands
- Clairvoyant abilities develop or expand
- Empathic abilities increase
- Clairaudient abilities develop or expand *
- Clairsentient abilities develop or expand †

As your crown chakra opens up, these abilities will start to manifest in different ways for each person. For instance, your clairvoyant abilities may be the most developed ability while, for someone else, clairaudient abilities may turn out to be that person's strongest gift. Everyone develops their own unique abilities.

Once your crown and third eye chakras have been properly activated and balanced, you will become fully psychic and more spiritually attuned. You will start to use even more of your brain capacity and easily switch back and forth from left- to right-brain thinking.

---

\*     I.e., abilities to hear sounds or voices psychically.

†     Empathic skills are only part of this: the ability to sense emotions and information from objects and people or to feel presences and energy encompasses this gift.

The ultimate purpose of all this is to become more enlightened in both a spiritual and humane way. With these abilities unfolding, it will be your mission in life to help yourself and others. Your soul within will become a beautiful light to others, helping to enlighten the souls of humankind.

# Chapter 4

# *The Human Aura*

> And after six days Jesus taketh Peter, James and
> John his brother, and bringeth them up into a
> high mountain apart, and was transfigured
> before them and his face did shine as the sun,
> and his raiment was white as the light.
> —Matthew 17:1–2

The human aura or energy field surrounding your body
has been written about since earliest times. The word aura
comes from the Latin word *aurum* meaning golden and the
Greek word *aura* meaning air or wind. It is sometimes also
called the electromagnetic field or the human energy field.

Human beings are composed of a duality, being both
physical and spiritual in nature: the physical being, the
body, exists at a lower rate of vibration; the spiritual being,
the psychic body and aura, exists in both the physical and
spiritual plane at a very high vibration.

Certain individuals who possess clairvoyant abilities can
observe the human aura or radiations of energy as multicolored lights enveloping the physical body, especially the
head. Through certain exercises and special visualization
techniques, you can be taught to sense or even see the aura.
The intent of this chapter and the following one is to teach
you to see as well as "read" auras.

# The Colors of the Aura

The multicolored lights surrounding the body are similar to the colors that are seen in a beautiful rainbow after a storm, or the illuminations of the Northern Lights on a wintry night. There are seven primary colors manifesting within the human aura. These colors are red, orange, yellow, green, blue, indigo, and purple. They are created by the magnetic field, the electric field, ultraviolet radiation, hormonal and chemical secretions, and spiritual energy.

Each one of these colors and their variations have a meaning. It is not enough for you to sense a human aura or energy field, you must also to be able to interpret the illuminations of colors. Known as "reading auras," this is an important skill that can help you in both your personal and professional relationships. The colors can be seen around the head and around the arms and hands of the individual being "read." This technique and its practice will be explained later in more detail.

Along with the seven main colors and their various hues there are also: gold, white, silver, gray, brown, and black. These luminations can be divided into two aspects, positive and negative; "positive" refers to good or beneficial colors, "negative" means bad or undesirable colors.

## Positive Colors

We will begin by discussing the beneficial or positive colors. These colors appear as pretty, clean, and clear luminations of energy. Simply put, they are pleasant to look at. People who cannot see the human aura can, in certain cases, feel or sense the colors. For example, someone may feel blue or green around people, and this translates to being comfortable and pleasant in their company.

The positive illumination of colors are as follows: light blue, mid blue, dark blue, light to mid green, sunshine or light yellow, light to mid orange, baby pink, medium to dark red, light purple, mid purple (indigo), silver, white, and gold.

These spiritual colors of the human aura field vibrate at a very high frequency. They cannot as yet be truly measured by any human technology.

### *True Positive Colors from High to Low Frequency (Vibratory Rate)*

- Light Blue
- Mid Blue
- Dark Blue
- Light to Mid Green
- Sunshine or Light Yellow
- Baby Pink
- Medium to Dark Red (Burgundy)

#### *Light Blue*
This beautiful lumination is similar to the blue of a summer afternoon sky.

This represents a loving and spiritual person, a peaceful individual. The more light blue present in a person's aura, the more loving and spiritual the person is. This color is a very high vibration of energy. Teachers, healers, and counselors who show compassion and love in their hearts for others will have this color prominently in their energy field.

This beautiful color can be seen or sensed around the head area. It completely envelops the head and ranges from a half inch to about six inches outwards from the body. The thicker and brighter the blue surrounding the head, the more spiritually advanced the individual.

This is one of the most important colors to look for in a person's aura. If you look above or around a person's head and "see" an abundance of this lumination, then you can feel comfortable about this individual. If you do not see any or very little light blue anywhere around the head, either close to the surface or further out, you should become cautious when dealing with the person whom you are observing or "reading."

### Mid Blue

This color is similar to the mid blue of the ocean. Mid blue is at a lower frequency than the previously mentioned light blue but it still vibrates at a high rate.

This shade of blue is normally perceived around the head but further out than the light blue. It emanates anywhere from about two-and-a-half inches to seven inches out from the surface of the head.

This color represents technical skills and management abilities. Technical writers, technicians, computer analysts, engineers, scientists, and medical doctors are some examples of those who will display this emanation.

Mid blue also signifies someone who is very practical and business oriented. Other individuals possessing this color prominently in their aura or energy field are accountants, business managers, office managers, sales managers, and business entrepreneurs.

Persons who have mid blue predominant in their aura, especially about the head, may not be employed in any of these careers. Yet, the presence of this color does mean that these individuals have certain characteristics or qualities dominant in their personality. These characteristics include a high potential for learning technical skills or a tendency to be very practical and business oriented. Individuals with mid blue predominant in their aura use the logical side or left hemisphere of their brains more than those with less mid blue.

The presence of the mid blue color will increase as an individual uses his or her technical skills and management abilities. In other words, the more a person employs his or her talent, the stronger and more expanded the mid blue color becomes within the auric field. The increase of this particular color is really noticeable about the head, shoulders, and arms after a person has been working for some time at a chore associated with his or her profession. When at rest or not involved in these types of careers, these individuals will still possess the mid blue color in their energy fields but at significantly lesser degrees.

### Dark Blue

This dark blue is similar to the deep blue seen in the sky close to evening. It is just slightly lighter than midnight blue. This emanation of light energy is at an above-medium rate of vibration or frequency, lower than the light blue color and just barely below the frequency of mid blue. It is a rich and beautiful color for the eyes to behold.

Persons possessing this color prominently in their auras are very creative and artistic in nature. The dark blue color can be seen or sensed around the subject's head, usually ranging anywhere from four to ten inches away from the surface. Writers, artists, craftspeople, painters, actors, dancers, and musicians are some examples of individuals with this lumination inherent in their human energy fields.

Once again, certain persons may have this color displayed in their auras but they many not be using these gifts. The presence of the color indicates a potential or tendency to be creative and artistic. Perhaps someone is employed as a grocery clerk, using his or her manual skills in a noncreative way, but he or she dreams of becoming a writer or poet. When this man or woman picks up a pen and starts to create the written word, the dark blue emanation within the energy field will greatly increase, particularly about the head area.

### Light to Mid Green

The light to mid green illumination is similar to the color of leaves in spring or of new grass in a park. The hue or tint of green of this important healing energy ranges between the two examples given above. It is at a fairly high rate of vibration or frequency, just slightly below the light blue color and slightly above the frequencies of mid blue and dark blue.

This color is associated with healing. Natural healers exhibit this green very prominently in their auras. It can usually be seen all over the head, very close to the hair or surface, and just above the shoulders and arms. It will also emanate from the hands. To a clairvoyant who sees the light to mid green color easily, the subject's hair will appear slightly green as if he or she has tinted their hair. You can develop healing gifts as well!

Some nurses, counselors, medical doctors, teachers, massage therapists, chiropractors, and other people whose careers are connected with the healing fields are ones who possess this beautiful green energy around them in most cases.

Once again, there are individuals who have natural healing energy but do not work in any healing profession. The light to mid green in their auras show the healing ability even though they are not using it. When a person *does* use his or her healing ability, the green color is amplified greatly during and after using the natural healing energy.

For example, a massage therapist who possesses the green healing color within his or her auric field will have this beautiful color displayed very prominently all about the head, the shoulders, upper and lower arms and hands, and fingers after finishing a massage treatment on a client.

Essentially, the light to mid green means two things. The person who possesses this color about his or her aura is either a healer or is in the process of being healed of an affliction. An individual who is sick, tired, in some discomfort or pain, or is simply at a low physical or emotional level may have this lumination contained within his or her energy field. The healing energy may appear about the head and shoulders areas, or be resident about a particular region of the body, usually where healing energy is being focused.

When "reading" the human aura, it is important to look at the hands of the subject. If the lumination of green is surrounding the hands, thumbs, and fingers and appears to radiate outwards, then the subject is healthy and his or her natural *chi* energy is flowing properly through most of the body. Conversely, if the subject's hands, fingers, and thumbs do not have any of this healing lumination present anywhere, then the subject has a health problem or the natural energy of the human body is not flowing properly.

The healer or potential healer will have this beautiful healing color all over the head, the shoulders, arms, and pouring forth from the hands. For the clairvoyant or aura reader who can see the human energy field, the person being observed or "read" will have this color as the main or most prominent color surrounding the body.

A person who is sick and has healing energy working through the body and aura will not have the green color as prominently displayed and he or she will have little or none of this energy emanating from the hands. This subject will be covered in more detail when we discuss negative or unhealthy colors of the human aura.

### Sunshine or Light Yellow

This color appears as very light yellow sunshine pouring through a window. It also looks like the bright radiation of a yellow tulip. It is very vibrant and pretty to gaze upon. The sunshine yellow's vibrating rate is at a midrange or frequency below the dark and mid blue colors.

Person's displaying this color prominently within their auric fields normally have positive, outgoing natures and high energy levels. It is a very clean, bright illumination that can be seen around the head area, usually an inch to four inches above the hair or surface of the head. It expands and contracts in width around the head according to the individual's state of mind, health condition, and physical stamina. The more sunshine yellow seen or sensed around a person, the more positive and "charged" the person is. Individuals such as comedians, extroverts, and true optimists will have a great amount of this energy within their auras.

The majority of humans possess amounts of this lumination in their energy fields in varying degrees. However, there are some people who have little or none of the yellow energy around their heads and physical bodies. These persons have some very negative qualities such as undesirable mental attitudes and low energy levels. This will be explained in greater detail when we discuss negative colors of the human aura.

### Baby Pink

The baby pink color is at a low to mid vibratory rate in the auric color scale. It is below the vibration or frequency of sunshine yellow. This lumination looks similar to the pretty pink in a baby blanket or sweater.

Individuals who have this pretty pink color in their auras are full of deep, universal love for humankind. This pastel lumination can be seen or sensed about eight to fourteen inches out from the surface of the head. It appears as pink lights swirling above and around the outskirts of the auric field.

People who give of themselves to help others have this lumination of universal love energy prevalent in their energy fields. The caring counselor, the loving social worker, or the friendly volunteer are prime examples. You have all met someone like this in your life.

These special people have an overconcern for others and a tendency to put their own needs and wants on hold. This can be detrimental to some of them if they do not learn to care for themselves as well.

### Medium to Dark Red (Burgundy)

This positive red color found in the auric field is at the lowest vibratory rate or frequency of all the positive colors. It appears as beautiful, rich burgundy emanations that you can see in a glass of red wine.

People possessing this rich, deep color in their auras have significant amounts of sexual energy. They are, in most cases, quite "lusty" in nature.

This illumination of energy can be seen around the head area, usually arranged in small clouds or blobs of deep red about three to seven inches out from the surface or hair. This sexual energy will also be seen throughout the "lusty" person's auric field. It will appear as wine or burgundy colored emanations around the shoulders, arms, hands, and legs.

The more "sexually charged" the person is, the more prominent the color is about the individual. In many cases, the medium or deep red lumination will appear over the chest and stomach areas as well. This energy will change in intensity according to the mood of the individual. If a person is sexually frustrated, this red energy will be seen or sensed mostly above the head and will be slightly lighter in color.

## Neutral Color

The following color is neither good nor bad in meaning. Of course, you may form your own opinion regarding this energy based on your own auric experiences.

### Honey or Golden Brown

Light honey brown is a neutral color that can sometimes enter into the human aura. If you were to take light chocolate and blend it in with golden honey, you would create the approximate hue of this neutral color. It is rather plain to look at.

Honey or golden brown represents power, wealth, and social position. It is neither positive nor negative in nature. It is a representation of earthly materialistic energy. Occasionally, politicians, lawyers, business executives, accountants, and wealthy merchants may have this illumination in their energy fields.

For the clairvoyant or aura reader, the honey or golden brown will be "seen" surrounding the head area completely and in some situations enveloping the entire body. Imagine a golden brown shroud of a see-through substance thrown over a person, completely filling the whole human aura. That's the way this honey-colored energy appears to people who possess the ability to see or sense it.

## Rare Positive Colors

As per the previous list of true positive colors, the rare ones are white, gold, light purple, mid purple (indigo), and light to mid orange. All of these special luminations of energy vibrate at a very high rate (frequency) except for the light to mid orange.

These rare colors are not seen or sensed in the human energy field as often as the regular positive ones. These high radiations of energy, excluding the light to mid orange, become more apparent within the individual's auric field as he or she becomes more spiritually and psychically awakened.

As our species evolves from Homo sapiens into Homo superior, more of you will have these colors of very high frequencies start residing within your human energy fields.

These are emanations of light that represent the true enlightenment of humankind. Powerful healers, great teachers, and gifted counselors in the future will work with these energies which literally descend from the heavenly realms and link with human auras.

### Rare Positive Colors from High to Low Frequency (Vibratory Rate)

- White
- Gold
- Silver
- Light Purple
- Mid Purple (Indigo)
- Light to Mid Orange

### White

This pure light is similar in whiteness to a white puffy cloud drifting by in a blue sky, except it displays more brilliance. If you can imagine the pure brightness of an angel's wings, then you can realize what this white light really looks like. With proper training and practice, you will be able to see this beautiful energy around more enlightened individuals. In the near future, more people will have this illumination of energy within their auras. The white light of pure energy is of the very highest vibratory rate.

This very special, pure energy originates from the higher realms or heavenly fields. If you were to study physics and the color spectrum, the color of white would be described as a combination of all colors. Scientifically, this may be true on a physical level, but this type of white light has greater ramifications: it goes far beyond the physical realm of our visible world.

This rare lumination of energy only resides in individuals who are on their true path in life or about to enter into it. As these people become more enlightened and more perceptive, they start to receive white light from the heavenly realms through their crown chakras. This beautiful light increases in strength as these special people start to fulfill their missions in life. The illumination slowly works through the human aura by first enveloping the head area and finally the whole auric field.

### Gold

This beautiful color is similar in appearance to the light yellow gold found in jewelry, except with more brilliance. It is an extremely high rate of vibration, second only to the pure energy of white light.

The color of gold represents wisdom and knowledge from a higher source, a higher dimension. Persons who display this color within their human energy fields are accessing information from a higher level. They are highly intuitive at times, very perceptive, and possess a sense of heightened awareness.

Gifted teachers and counselors are prime examples of people who have gold energy around them. This golden light is not always apparent within the auras of such people. It becomes more visible and amplifies in width and intensity when they teach and counsel others using their special psychic abilities.

This color can usually be seen about seven to twelve inches above the head in the outer area of the crown chakra. In some rare cases, golden energy will completely encompass the head and body of an individual who is more enlightened.

There have been references made in religious and spiritual literature to "the Golden Bowl," "the Golden Halo," and "the Crown of Gold." Even some of our religious works by artists such as Da Vinci, Raphael, and Giotto show auras or "golden halos" around the heads of religious figures. These are simply examples of human auras when gold energy becomes predominant.

### Silver

This silver illumination is similar to silver jewelry as it reflects the sunlight. If you can think of the pure white light with a light gray mixed in, you can get a better understanding of this color. This silver energy can be seen or sensed around the head, about one to three inches out from the surface. It represents a very high rate of vibration, just below the gold color and is pleasant to gaze upon.

The color of silver represents psychic and spiritual awakening. Individuals who are becoming more aware of their mission or purpose in life start to display this lumination in their human energy fields.

People who feel empty, unfilled in their life and careers, and are searching for more purpose to their existence also have the silver emanation in their auras. These awakening souls develop a sincere desire to serve others and make a difference in the world. Many persons who experience a major midlife career change and senior citizens who give of their time to charity are a few examples of those who also have this color in their energy fields.

### Light Purple

The light purple lumination is similar to the mauve-like color of lilacs and is very beautiful to gaze upon. This emanation of psychic and spiritual energy vibrates at a very high frequency, just below the gold and silver colors. It is created by the mixing of light blue and mid purple (indigo).

This beautiful pastel color represents a combination of psychic abilities and spiritual enlightenment. People who possess the light purple color in their auras are fairly psychic, with a spiritual depth to them. They will often use their psychic gifts in a spiritual, loving, and caring way.

Intuitive counselors, spiritual teachers, spiritual advisors, and religious leaders are some of the people who display this lumination in their energy fields. Others who have deep, religious faiths or spiritual beliefs can sometimes have the light purple color around them.

Individuals who are developing their psychic abilities and are on a spiritual quest will begin to display this pretty color in their auras. They may add purple- or mauve-colored clothing to their wardrobe as they show a new liking or affinity with this color. For most, this change will occur without any conscious knowledge of the change.

The more spiritual and psychic the person is, the more light purple will be displayed in the auric field around the head area. It can usually be "seen" or sensed in the crown chakras (top of the head) and the third eye chakras (forehead). In some situations, this energy will make the hair on the head appear tinted light purple.

### Mid Purple (Indigo)

The mid purple or indigo energy is similar to the color of an amethyst crystal but with more luminance. Its vibratory rate (frequency) is very high compared to normal, positive colors, but slightly below the silver and light purple emanations.

This dark, beautiful color indicates psychic abilities and psychic power. This particular illumination is fully representative of psychic gifts only. Unlike the light purple color, mid purple does not represent a spiritual element or a spiritual use of the psychic gifts.

Individuals who have the mid purple or indigo color manifested in their auric fields are very psychic in nature, but not necessarily spiritual. They normally use their abilities such as intuition to seek answers psychically for themselves and others.

Clairvoyants, psychics, aura readers, past life regressionists and some sales and business-oriented people with psychic gifts are prime examples of human beings who have this illumination of energy around them. Other people using the mid purple energy come from all walks of life; they employ their gifts to help themselves, family members, and friends.

The more mid purple (indigo) color you "see" around a person's head, the more psychically developed that person is. Like the light purple color, it will be seen or sensed in the crown chakra and third eye chakra. This energy may also completely envelope the entire head and shoulders, close to the surface and expanding four inches outwards from the body.

### Light to Mid Orange
If you picture an orange on a tree with the sun glistening on it, then you will see how this bright, positive color truly appears.

Unlike the rest of the rare positive colors, the light to mid orange illumination is at a lower vibratory rate, just slightly below the normal sunshine or light yellow color.

Light to mid orange represents creative humor.

Gifted comedians and witty storytellers have this orange color either within their auric field or just slightly outside it. This color appears as a light to mid orange ball of energy to a clairvoyant or aura reader. It usually hovers about ten to twelve inches above and off to the side of the head, just outside of the auric field. When a comedian or other funny person employs their gift of humor, this energy then enters into the aura through the crown chakras. In rare instances, this color will remain within the energy field.

## Shifting of the Auric Colors

Always remember that the positive or beneficial colors of the human aura look very clear, clean, and beautiful. The aura and the colors within it expand and contract constantly. These luminations of energy shift and move about much like the colors of the Northern Lights in the night sky. They swirl and mix together about the body.

Therefore, keep in mind that the location of these true colors is approximate and can slowly shift about.

In the past, many teachers and writers of esoteric knowledge have made references to the human energy field as being subdivided into different layers or bodies. For simplicity's sake, we treat the aura here as one complete system that surrounds the human body.

> The Northern Lights dance and swirl in the
> midnight sky. The seven colors of the rainbow
> radiate beauty. The human aura is an expres-
> sion of both.
> —Douglas De Long

## Negative Colors

In contrast with the positive auric colors, the negative or
undesirable colors that do sometimes appear within the
human aura (but are not normally inherent to it), are
black, gray, dirty yellow, dirty orange, brown, bright pink,
light red, reddish purple, and dark green. These colors
appear as ugly, dirty, or mucky luminations of energy that
are not pleasant to perceive.

Negative or undesirable colors appear in the aura under
various conditions. Negative emotions such as fear, anger,
worry, and sadness can affect the aura by changing the colors in it and introducing negative energy at the same time.
Minor illnesses such as a cold or flu will also be expressed
within the human energy field as cloudy, unpleasant colors.
Tiredness and lack of energy can be seen or sensed in the
aura. Personality faults and bad mental attitudes are certain
characteristics that can appear within the aura as well.

Negative colors in the aura are of a much lower frequency or rate of vibration than the positive ones. It is sufficient for you to understand that these dirty and unwanted
luminations are of a lower vibratory rate, they vary only in
their expression of dirtiness and ugliness.

## Negative Colors from High to Low Frequency (Vibratory Rate)

- Black
- Gray
- Dirty Yellow
- Dirty Orange
- Dull Brown
- Dirty Brown
- Bright Pink
- Light Red
- Reddish Purple
- Dark Green

### Black

This energy is the exact opposite of the white light of pure energy. It is a very dirty and heavy lumination that has different meanings depending on where it is located within the human aura. The more apparent the black color is in the aura, the more intense the problem or situation is.

People who think very negatively or who are deceitful have this ugly color strongly entrenched in their auric fields, usually surrounding the head area and in many cases covering the rest of the body like a shroud. Usually their auric fields are fairly strong but appear polluted. These are the individuals to beware of. In business and in personal relationships, they will not be loyal or trustworthy. Some may have a tendency to lie, tell partial truths, and be deceitful towards others. These people do not like themselves and may mirror their feelings of dislike and negativity onto close friends and relatives. In certain cases, these individuals may be verbally, emotionally, or physically abusive towards their spouses or intimate partners. They have very little positive energy showing around their heads.

Under certain conditions you may even be able to tell when another person is lying to you, deceiving you. This will be fully explained in chapter 5, "Reading the Human Aura."

If certain persons appear or "feel" like their auric fields are close about them and a light black with less density is around their heads (usually about two or four inches out from the surface), then they are tired and possibly depressed. These individuals may still have some positive colors showing in their auras, especially about the head, but intermingled with the light black energy.

For counselors and others versed in the studies of human nature, the following example of another manifestation of this negative color can help immensely in treating certain people. If you gaze at a person's face and it appears to be covered in a grayish black shroud of energy, making it difficult to clearly see the face, then that person has experienced excessive abuse in his or her life. A portion of this abuse may have originated from earlier times.

This unhappy soul has been on the receiving end of emotional, verbal, or physical abuse for some time. He or she needs counseling in order to break the cycle of abuse from the past as it carries over into the present.

By recognizing this dirty or "yucky" emanation of negative energy, you can learn to help others and protect yourself. The black color of a low vibratory rate feels oppressive and uncomfortable to sensitive people and empaths.

### Gray

The negative color of gray in the human aura has the same meaning as black energy, but to a lesser degree. It can also indicate that someone is sick. For instance, if a grayish swirl of energy is seen or sensed in the forehead area, localized over the left eyebrow, then this person has a headache in that area.

To a clairvoyant, these people with gray in their auras look like they need to take a shower or a bath.

### Dirty Yellow

Dirty yellow within the human energy field is easy to distinguish from sunshine yellow. It looks like a beautiful yellow color with mud or charcoal dust mixed into it. This lumination of negative energy is ugly in appearance.

Dirty yellow is an indication of energy blocks in the body and aura that result in health problems. Someone suffering from an illness or disease will have this unclean color within the energy field, usually in front of the problem area. Once you learn to "see" or sense the colors of the human aura, you can tell if someone has certain health problems. For example, a woman suffering from the early to midstages of breast cancer will have this dirty yellowish color floating and shifting just in front of the breast. People with arthritic conditions also manifest this same energy around the afflicted areas such as shoulders, wrists, finger joints, and knees. Someone with back problems such as sciatica pain running down the legs will have a streak of dirty yellow flowing down one or both legs, depending on the severity of the pain. If a green color seems to blend in with the yellow then healing energy is working through the nerves and other afflicted regions. The appearance of this green healing color anywhere in the aura where the dirty yellow resides also indicates that the human body is trying to heal this region.

On a more positive note, active individuals who have just exerted some of their muscles will show a slightly lighter version of this yellow energy over the particular muscle groups that have been exerted.

Even though this is a negative, unclean energy of low vibration, it can be used as a valuable healing tool by indicating potentially serious health conditions within the body before the illness becomes too advanced. In certain situations, an aura reader or clairvoyant will see the illness within the aura prior to it manifesting in the body. This can be a marvelous preventative tool for the healing fields if its true value is recognized.

### Dirty Orange

The unclean negative energy of dirty orange means the same as dirty yellow except with more intensity. In other words, this undesirable color indicates that the illness or injury is more progressed or advanced. This ugly orange energy can be a sign of a cancer or other serious illness which can be reversed only with difficulty.

### Dull Brown

The dull, negative color of brown can indicate different conditions depending on where the brown lumination is perceived in the human energy field.

If the brown energy completely surrounds the head area (and in certain individuals, the rest of the body), then they are very negative, deceitful, and are generally characters of very low ethical standards and morals. This unpleasant energy appears as a solid but light chocolate color in the outer areas of the aura radiating inwards but remaining several inches away from the surface of the head and body.

Sexual perverts, pedophiles, psychopathic killers, dangerous persons, corrupt and unethical business people, and other unwanted "dregs of society" are examples of persons who manifest this type of brown energy.

Please, do not confuse this terrible color with the following negative aspect of brown.

### Dirty Brown

Individuals who have a dirty brown color manifested within their energy fields are very seriously ill. In many cases, this can indicate advanced cancer in the human body. Death is very near at hand for these souls. The dirty energy will normally hover above the diseased area of the human body, shifting and swirling about.

If a person with cancer suffers from the disease throughout his or her body, the negative energy of brown will hover and swirl throughout the whole human aura. It will look as if someone threw brown muck and charcoal dust into the aura.

This dirty brown color reflects the progression of an illness or disease from its early stages indicated by dirty yellow energy. As an individual becomes sicker, his or her aura will show the yellow color slowly changing to dirty orange and finally to dirty brown.

For sensitive or empathic people, the human energy fields of severely ill persons will feel weak, draining, and uncomfortable to be near.

### Bright Pink

Bright pink is a glaring energy that is unattractive to see or sense.

Picture a gentle, pastel, or "baby" pink color blended with a more intense, harsher hue of red. For some of you this hue of pink will appear unpleasing, even ugly. The color is a combination of soft brightness and angry intensity.

Argumentative people have bright pink residing within their auric fields. This bright but ugly illumination of energy is normally seen or sensed either partially or fully surrounding the head area, three to six inches out from the surface. Extremely argumentative persons will appear to have this angry color completely encircling their heads. You should avoid such people whenever possible. In rare circumstances, this color will appear as a small cloud floating over the heart area.

### Light Red

Light red represents anger, frustration and in some situations, energy blocks in the body.

Individuals who have this illumination of energy contained within their energy fields on a semipermanent basis are full of deep-seated anger and frustration and in some cases, rage. They have not fully dealt with and released their anger and other negative emotions in a manner that would heal their emotions. They are like a pent-up emotional volcano, ready to erupt. For these volatile people, the red lumination is very pronounced above and off to the side of the head. It may also appear over the heart area. It hovers like a small red cloud in these two areas, looking angry and ugly.

Unhealthy emotions such as pent-up anger will slowly and ultimately manifest into energy blocks, then appear as physical blocks or other problems.

People suffering from certain heart conditions will have a very light red color manifest over the heart and sometimes the whole chest region; also over the left shoulder and left upper arm. If the condition is dormant or controlled, the light red energy will be barely visible above the heart. If the heart condition is active, the light red energy will spread across the chest.

Light red can also be seen in joints and muscles that have been injured or diseased. For instance, someone suffering from a very sore shoulder or arthritic affliction here will have an ugly light to slightly darker light red color manifest directly over the shoulder close to the surface of the skin.

Even though the light red represents energy blocks and health problems and the slightly darker light red represents anger, both shades of this lumination indicate anger. It can be an emotional anger within a person or simply a muscle, tendon, or other "angry" body part.

If you are observing an individual who usually has positive colors in his or her aura, but then begins to exhibit red clouds of energy manifesting on either side of the head and over the heart area, then this person has just become angry. As this anger is released and the individual returns to a state of calm, the red color in his or her aura will dissipate.

Being able to see or sense this negative color of a lower vibration is helpful for healing and counseling.

### Reddish Purple

Earlier, we discussed the rare, positive colors that can start to show in the human aura. Light purple or mauve color indicating both psychic and spiritual awakening and mid purple or indigo referring to psychic abilities exclusively. The reddish purple color is dirtier and angrier looking than positive purple energy. If you can imagine mid purple being smeared together with angry light red, you get the general idea of the true color of this negative energy. This lumination is perceived on top of the head in the crown chakra and in the forehead within the third eye chakra. It may also cover the surface of the head and make the hair appear to be tinted with this ugly color.

A reddish purple color within the human aura means both psychic abilities and anger. Individuals displaying this negative energy within their auras are fairly psychic but are full of anger and frustration. For these persons, releasing anger or other negative emotions will trigger and enhance psychic abilities within. Unusual psychic phenomena may happen at this time, such as glasses breaking or objects moving by themselves. Telekinetic powers (such as the ability to move objects by thought alone) are but one example of the psychic manifestation of these emotions.

These individuals may possess unique psychic abilities but tend to use them in a negative manner. However, once these people let go of their anger and become more peaceful, their psychic abilities may start to become true gifts.

### Dark Green

The undesirable color of dark green has nothing in common with the positive green that represents healing. Mix the mid green color of summer grass and charcoal dust together and you will have an approximation of this dirty, negative energy. It appears as a grayish, mid green color in the form of an energy cloud. This unpleasant energy surrounds all or part of the head area of the human energy field, ranging about four to seven inches out from the surface.

People who have this negative lumination within their auric fields are generally jealous and envious of others. They have a tendency to covet what others have. This character flaw may range from petty jealousy directed at a co-worker to lusting after someone else's spouse or lover. The stronger this negative green color is in the human aura, the more jealous or envious in nature is the person.

## The Colors of the Universe

In this chapter, the colors of the human aura have been covered in order to help you be able to interpret their true meanings as you start to see and sense them around others in the very near future.

The ultimate goal of reading or interpreting a human energy field is to help others. *Summum bonum*, the Latin expression meaning "the supreme or highest good," applies to the art and expertise of reading the human aura.

Please consult appendix 2 at the end of this book (page 235 and following) for a complete chart of the colors of the human aura, their meaning, and location around the body.

> The colors of the universe are within you.
> You are one with the rainbow in the sky.
> —Douglas De Long

# Chapter 5

# *Reading and Interpreting the Human Aura*

The hand of God painted the sky with the
colors of the rainbow in all their radiance.
—Douglas De Long

The ability to read and interpret the colors of the human
aura can prove to be invaluable as a preventative and diag-
nostic tool in the health field, an interpretive mechanism in
the field of counseling and as a way to obtain an accurate
insight into personal and business relationships. In the near
future, our society will start to recognize the importance of
the illuminations of the human energy field and utilize this
knowledge in order to help humankind.

Professional aura readers and medical intuitives, clairvoyants who use their gifts to "read" health problems in
people's auras will be in greater demand as more holistic
therapies arise and become more common.

This chapter is dedicated to special techniques for helping you start to see and read the human auric field accurately. For those of you who can already see the auric colors,
these techniques or exercises will enhance this attribute.

Combining this ability with a thorough understanding of what these colors mean will allow you to become proficient as an aura reader, either professionally or privately.

## Toning Techniques

In chapters 2 and 3, special vowel intonations were given to you. Both the intonations of Thoh and May are important sounds for developing or enhancing your ability to see auras.

As explained, the Thoh chant is an initial one time only exercise to be practiced and then forgotten for a long time. The May chant, on the other hand, was given to you as a special technique to be used on a regular basis.

Prior to attempting to see a person's aura, the proper toning of M-a-y should be done two or three times. This helps to slow down your brain wave patterns from a beta waking state to an alpha or slightly altered state. You should not do this exercise more than twice in one day. If you chant M-a-y more than two times in a day, you will become very light-headed and spacy, and may even get a headache.

When you are first learning how to see the human aura, the toning of M-a-y should become a part of your daily regimen. Eventually, as you become more adept at seeing and sensing auras, the practice of chanting becomes less important. Instead of toning M-a-y before you begin, you can simply do it whenever you wish. Sometimes once or twice a week is sufficient as you start to enter altered states more easily.

After completing the May exercise, you can move on to the next preparatory technique.

# Breathing Techniques

Proper breathing techniques are important. Most individuals have a tendency to breathe in a shallow manner. If you can get into the habit of taking in deeper breaths, your health and energy level will improve.

Prior to "reading" or seeing the aura around a person, deep breathing should be done in a particular way. Take a deep breath in slowly through your nose, feeling your chest and diaphragm expanding. Focus on your chest, first letting it start to expand, then move your attention to the diaphragm below, allowing the air entering the lungs to also fill the lower area. It should feel like your whole chest and upper abdomen is filling with air. Once you have inhaled as much air as possible, hold your breath for about five seconds. Feel the breath within. Finally, release your breath slowly out through both your nose and mouth in a gentle, constant motion, until all the breath has left your lungs. Repeat this whole process a second time; if you desire, you can even repeat it a third time.

The reason for this breathing technique is that there is spirit energy (also known as *chi*, life force, or Universal Energy) in the air that we breathe and all around us in nature. This energy comes from the God source, the Creator, and the heavenly fields above. When it enters into our earthly realm, it permeates everything: the rocks, the trees, the seas, and the air that we breathe.

By breathing in air, you bring the spirit energy into your lungs. Holding your breath for approximately five seconds allows the spirit energy or life force to circulate through your body. Once the life force is within your body, your own auric field starts to expand, your heart rate and breathing slow down, and ultimately, your brainwave patterns slow down into a light trance or alpha state. This creates a heightened state of consciousness, making it easier for you to see auras and higher energy vibrations. You are now ready for the next step.

## Wall or Background Technique

Place a chair against a light-colored wall. Later, you can experiment with different colored walls ranging from white to dark. For the best result, adjust the lighting to resemble a near-dusk environment. Trying this wall or background technique is easier in the day than at night. However, if you are attempting this in the evening after sunset, you can use candles and soft light in the distance to resemble a near-dusk setting.

Have a volunteer or subject sit in the chair facing you. There should be about five to ten feet between you and your volunteer. Take some relaxing breaths. Have your volunteer do the same. Following this, both of you should return to normal breathing. Ask your volunteer to stare off into space. He or she should relax and not attempt to do anything but sit there, unconcerned.

When you have your volunteer take some deep breaths in and relax, his or her aura will expand greatly. This makes it easier for you to notice the white light or emanation.

Now, gaze about the head of the person sitting in the chair. Your gaze should be relaxed, almost unfocused, on the wall behind the subject's head. Allow yourself to stare "through the wall" as if you are looking at something in the distance. Do not try to see or look for the aura around the

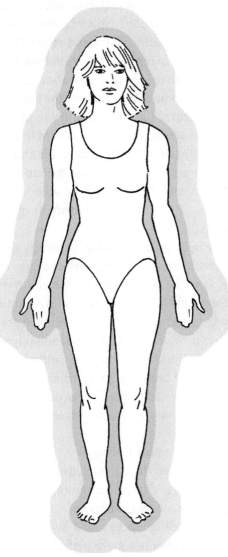

Human energy field (i.e., aura) surrounding a woman.

volunteer. Keep staring through the wall. As you continue to do this in a relaxed state, you will start to see a white light or energy emanation above and around the subject's head. At this point, bring your attention back from staring "through the wall" to glancing just above the head. You should continue to be able to observe the light around the subject's head providing you do not try to focus too hard on what you are seeing. If you try too hard to see the aura, you will lose sight of it. It takes some time and practice to learn how to train your eyes to see the emanation on a steady basis. Eventually, you will be able to allow your vision to become slightly out of focus to observe auras around others.

The white light or illumination of energy that you see around your subject is not the pure white energy mentioned previously. It is the beginning of your ability to see the human energy field. This is an excellent start onto the path of aura reading. Eventually, through continued practice, you will begin to see colors about the head and body.

For the professional aura reader or medical intuitive, the energy around the head area provides about sixty percent of the information that is needed for diagnosis. This area should be one of your main focal points when reading and interpreting auras.

A variation of the Wall Technique is the use of a black or dark cloth placed onto the wall directly behind the subject's head. Sometimes, a darker background enables you to notice the aura or energy field easier.

Practice the Wall or Background Technique whenever possible. Practice does not make perfect, but it does make you better at seeing auras. For fun, try switching positions with your subject. It may be even more enjoyable to try this experiment with a friend or relative.

If you already see auras, this technique will enhance your ability. Some individuals can see auras all the time in both daylight and near-dark situations. Many children can do this instinctively, thanks to their natural psychic openness.

## Tree Gazing Technique

Everything in nature is surrounded by energy patterns—animals, plants, rocks, and trees.

The indigenous peoples of North America believe that Mother Earth and all her inhabitants are alive, animate objects. For example, through both their culture and language, the Cree refer to a rock as an animate object. Trees are also a part of this spiritual belief.

Keeping this thought in mind will help you with the Tree Gazing Technique. Even though the best time to try tree gazing is before, during and just after sunset, this particular exercise can be done anytime of day: morning, afternoon, evening, or even late at night. As the sun starts to set, the energy of the earth starts to shift and change. The electro-magnetic energy and spirit energy that is within all living things starts to increase. The air itself is charged with higher vibratory rates of energy similar to the atmosphere immediately following a thunderstorm. These conditions create the ideal situation for seeing light or energy around trees.

Before you attempt the Tree Gazing Technique, get yourself comfortable, take two or three relaxing breaths, and then return to normal breathing. Focus on a tree of your choice. Keep focusing your gaze directly at the tree for a few seconds, then look above or around the tree, allowing your eyes to start looking past the tree. Soon, you will start to notice a slight white light or blue white light surrounding the tree like a silhouette. Now bring your attention back to above or around the tree, allowing yourself to remain calm and peaceful. If your are successful, you will still be able to see the emanation of energy around the tree. You are now in an altered state, a heightened state of awareness, and are seeing the higher vibrations of energy including the aura or energy field around the tree that you chose as your subject.

Try this technique at nighttime as well as at sunset. When you do this, you are training yourself to slow down your brainwaves and to see energy fields. If you like, a large bush may be substituted for the tree. Ultimately, you will begin to see energy around other things in nature.

## Candle and Mirror Technique

This particular technique should be practiced in a dark room. Nighttime is preferable, but you can simulate this by closing curtains and blinds.

### Phase One

Once you have created a nighttime atmosphere, take two white or light colored candles and place them on a dresser or platform standing in front of a large mirror. Light both candles and position them on either side of the mirror out of your direct line of sight. Gaze at your reflection, noticing where there is too much shadow on your face. Adjust the candles to remove as much of the shadow as possible and to allow the candlelight to show your head, face, and shoulders clearly reflected in the mirror.

After the candles have been positioned properly, start gazing directly into your eyes in the reflection. As you do this, let your gaze "look through" your eyes. Take deep, relaxing breaths. Three or four deep breaths should be sufficient. Remember to breathe in through your nose, filling both your chest and abdomen, and then let your breath out slowly, either through your mouth or nose. After three or four deep breaths, return to normal breathing again, still staring through your eyes into the distance. Your eyes and face may start to shift and change at his time. For example, your nose may look like it is getting longer or your eyes start to look different. This is expected as you enter into a deeper state of concentration.

You are now in the proper altered state to experiment with Phase Two of the Candle and Mirror Technique.

## Phase Two

Bring your focus back from staring "through your eyes" to staring at them, then lift your gaze above the head area of your reflection. Keep your gaze focused about one to three inches above the head. Try not to see anything, just allow events to unfold. If you are successful, you will see the energy emanation surrounding your whole head and even your shoulders. It will appear as a silhouette of white or light blue light expanding out from the head for a distance of one to four inches approximately.

You are now starting to see your own aura or energy field. A few of you who are "more opened" will see the beautiful colors of the aura swirling around your reflection in the mirror. This is the ultimate goal of this exercise.

After you have tried both phases of the Candle and Mirror Technique a few times, you can try to see and read your own aura about your head. Simply eliminate Phase One of the exercise and go to Phase Two directly.

As you observe your own energy about your head, try taking in a deep breath, holding it for about five seconds, and then release it slowly and evenly. Pay attention to your aura as you do this. You may notice the energy field about your head starting to expand. The human energy field is no different from other energy fields in that it can expand under certain conditions. As explained earlier, the chi or spirit energy entering your lungs and working through your whole body can expand or increase your auric field. By observing your energy about you as you do the breathing exercise, you may actually be able to see this phenomenon occurring.

Once you have completed the deep breathing and aura expanding experiment, try to focus all your attention above your head in the crown chakra area, about one inch above the top of the head. Imagine someone or something touching your scalp and hair. Feel the energy sensations and pressure there. In your mind, imagine a light or energy on top of your head. See this energy starting to push upward from the crown chakra or top of your head. Visualize and feel this energy expanding above and around your head area.

Now, gaze at your reflection in the mirror above your head. You should notice a visible change. The white or light blue emanation around your head should have expanded outwards several more inches.

The more you practice, the easier it will be for you to see your own energy field. Later, you can try both Phases One and Two of the Candle and Mirror Technique without the candles if you wish. Just use a mirror and make sure that you create a near-dusk environment in the room where you are. Too much external light or sunlight can make it difficult for you to see your aura.

Learning to see your own energy in a mirror will become increasingly natural for you as you practice these exercises.

## Candle Gazing Technique

For this technique, you need one white or light-colored candle in a holder. (The candle should not have a strong or dark color, because colored candles have a slightly different vibration of energy that can sometimes interfere with the desired results.)

Make sure the room is dark. Put the candle in its holder on top of any flat surface: a dresser, end tables, or even the floor may be used.

Light the candle, then find a comfortable place to sit, making sure that you are about five feet away from the candle. Take a few deep, relaxing breaths, then return to normal breathing, focusing on the lighted candle. Let your eyes stare through the flame. Now, move your eyes off to the side of the flame, just on the perimeter of the lumination. Start to focus your attention around the flame's edges. Pay attention to the different colors or hues that are present on the extreme edges of the flame.

The next part of this Candle Gazing Technique can be quite interesting. The colors red, orange, yellow, green, and blue should be used.

As you continue observing the energy and colors around the outer edges, start to picture the color red in your head and then "project" the red color to the outer area of the flame. Visualize this energy flickering and shifting about the perimeter, completely surrounding the light. The red energy will actually start to manifest on the edges of the candle flame. It should become stronger in intensity as you continue gazing, thinking of red light. If you have difficulty in picturing red in your mind, try to think of a red fire truck. This approach can be used for any or all of the colors. Picturing green grass or green trees in your mind, for example, will allow the green energy to manifest in your mind and finally about the exterior of the flame.

As you see the lumination of red forming around the edges, you may think that this is your imagination creating the phenomenon. In reality, you are actually causing the manifestation by changing the vibrations of energy about the candlelight with the power of your thoughts, your mind. In essence, you are directing red energy from the universe into the room.

This is a powerful technique that can be used to help heal disease and the suffering of humankind. Eventually, you will be able to manifest and direct different healing colors into a person's aura and body. Very soon, our society will be using colors, sounds, vibrations, and crystals for healing purposes.

After manifesting the color of red, repeat the experiment in the same manner, using orange, yellow, green, and blue, respectively.

Practice the Candle Gazing Technique until you become proficient at it. This exercise enables certain areas of your brain to awaken, letting abilities such as clairvoyance and aura reading to come forth.

## Sunset Gazing Technique

This is a fairly easy, straightforward technique to try. Many people do not take time to enjoy beautiful sunsets, instead taking them for granted.

If you can get into the habit of watching beautiful sunsets while in a peaceful, relaxed frame of mind, you will enter into deep, altered states of consciousness much more easily and quickly, as desired.

Get yourself into a comfortable position. Take two or three deep breaths. Start gazing at the sunset, noticing the various colors and hues in the sky. Pay special attention to the many colors that are seen in the cloud formations. Just watch and enjoy the scene unfolding before you. Let all of your attention be directed to watching the sunset, letting yourself drift with the beautiful clouds. These colors that you are enjoying are very similar in appearance to the colors of the human aura. When you recognize and appreciate the beauty inherent within a sunset, you also start to understand and appreciate the radiance of a person's auric field. There is a realization that the universe, nature, and human beings are all one.

One note of caution when practicing this technique: sustained, direct gazing at the sun can cause permanent loss of sight and other damage to the eyes. Please be careful to wait until the sun's light has diminished from its full intensity.

> Constantly regard the universe as one living
> being, having one substance and one soul.
>           —Marcus Aurelius (Roman emperor
>           and philosopher, 121–180 c.e.)

## Aura Reading Technique

Reading or interpreting an aura should not be done in a haphazard way. You need to develop a certain method or pattern of reading the energy around others. Be sure to use your intuition and sensitivity throughout the aura reading session.

In most situations, you should begin by reading the colors around the head area. As mentioned before, much of the information you need can be seen here. Remember to check the crown chakra and third eye chakra as you focus on the head area. Take your time seeing and sensing the colors of the aura here. Observe if the luminations are clean or dirty looking. Pay particular attention to how you feel about this person that is sitting before you. Empathy or sensitivity gives you an additional tool to use in accurately reading the aura. If you wish to, you can keep a pen and notebook beside you, jotting down what you see and sense around the head area. You can always refer back to your notes in order to assist yourself and your subject or volunteer. You can write down information throughout the entire reading.

After you have finished gazing at the head area, move down to the shoulders, observing and perceiving both positive and negative colors. Notice or sense if the energy in one shoulder is different than the other shoulder. If there appears to be a negative energy or something "feels" wrong in one of the shoulders, check with your subject for verification. Many people store tension in this area of the body. You will learn to tell this as you become more proficient at aura reading.

Next, move your gaze down both arms slowly and stop around the elbows, looking for any negative energy in these regions. After "reading" the elbows, continue moving your gaze down the forearms, looking for either green healing energy or energy blocks. Finally, stop your gazing eyes at the hands. The hands are a very important part of the body. By "reading" the colors around the hands and wrists, you can tell if the person is sick, if there are energy blocks in the body and its meridians, or if he or she is a natural healer. Even arthritis conditions can be spotted in the hands and wrists. If you pay close attention to how your

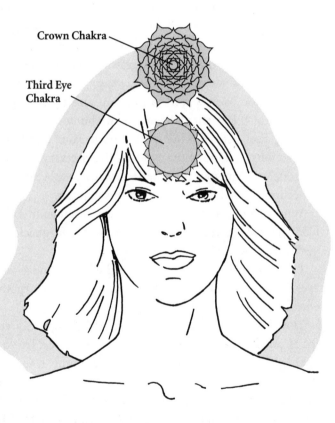

Crown Chakra

Third Eye
Chakra

**Illustration of an aura around a person's head and shoulders. When observing an aura, make sure that there is a wall or backdrop behind your subject.**

feel when focusing on the subject's hands, you can tell if the individual "feels" sick. If you are having trouble seeing the colors at first, do not be discouraged; just let yourself sense the color and energy. You can even use your "third eye" or "inner vision" to perceive the appropriate colors about your subject.

When using your "third eye" or "inner vision," you simply look inside your mind. You can keep your eyes open and remain staring at the hands or any other area of the human body as you allow your consciousness to go within your head. It is very similar to daydreaming. If you wish, you can close your eyes for a moment and focus in your mind upon the particular part of the body that you are reading. Feel, see, or sense the colors in your mind. The impressions or visions that you receive are very real and accurate. It is not your imagination! Many people can learn to accurately read human auras in this manner.

While reading and sensing the energy about your volunteer's hands, feel free to ask him or her for feedback and verification on what you see and sense.

Upon completing the reading of the hands, move your eyes up to the neck and throat area, looking for negative energy or dirty colors here.

Now, move your gaze down to the chest area. As you focus on the chest and especially the heart area, let your gaze "go through" the chest onto a focal point in the distance. As you are staring through the chest, watch the colors and energy forming around the chest. Refer back to the chart on auric colors in chapter 4 if you need to. This method is similar to using your peripheral vision for watching or observing.

After observing the energy or luminations in the chest, move your attention down to the abdomen, keeping your gaze above the navel region. Use the same gazing technique that you used while reading the chest area. Sense or see the energy blocks that may be here. It may appear as a grayish cloud floating over the abdomen. If so, then you are "reading" an energy block and possibly a health problem directly below the negative gray-colored cloud.

As a final step, do a quick reading on your volunteer's hips and legs. Ask your subject to stand up for a moment with his or her arms held slightly away from the body. Gaze along the sides of both hips slowly, and then move your eyes slowly down the outer side of one leg until you reach the foot, then the outer side of the other leg, moving from the hips and thighs downward. Take your time and do allow yourself to focus briefly upon the knees as you do your "hips and legs gazing." If you see or perceive negative energy or colors in one or both knees, then there is an energy block there, either in one or both knees. Once again, verify this with your subject.

You can even have your subject turn to face away from you so that you can read the energy that is in front of the spinal column, back, and buttocks. Negative colors seen or sensed over the spine can sometimes indicate disc problems with the back or even multiple sclerosis. If a light green color is perceived in any of the above mentioned areas, then healing energy is being directed into a part of the body that has an energy block and physical problem.

In certain situations, when you are asking for verification of what you see or sense, your subject may not be aware of any physical problems or blocks. This does not mean that you are wrong and that there is no problem in a certain area of your volunteer's body. It may mean that your subject is not aware of the condition or the negative energy is still in the auric field and has not yet manifested into the physical body.

Eventually, your aura reading subjects and volunteers will become your clients or patients in the future (if you intend to become a medical intuitive or professional aura reader). As you develop this useful gift, you can help friends and family members by diagnosing medical and emotional problems in their auric fields. For those of you who are in the medical and counseling fields this ability can further enhance your effectiveness. After all, your true purpose in life is to help others.

Nothing is impossible to a willing heart.
—Francis Bacon (British philosopher and scientist, 1561–1626)

# Chapter 6

# *The Chakra System*

The light of the Creator shines in the light of
you.
—Douglas De Long

The human energy field or aura that surrounds both the
physical body and the psychic body also contains many
energy centers within. These energy centers are called
chakras, from the Sanskrit word meaning "wheel of light."
This is a very apt description.

There are almost 130 energy centers associated with the
human body and found within the aura. Most of these
chakras are minor energy centers and are linked to parts of
the body such as the hands, knees, and feet. Seven of these
chakras or energy centers are major chakras, which are very
important for all human beings. The major chakras are
closely associated with the endocrine glandular system of
the body. They are located up and down the center of the
body and in the head (see the illustration on page 99). The
energy from these centers expands outwards from the
physical form. These seven major energy centers have specific names, and colors, and correspond to specific glands
and areas of the body. The following chart provides this
information.

| Chakra | Name | Color | Gland |
|--------|------|-------|-------|
| 7 | Crown | Light Purple | Pituitary |
| 6 | Brow, Third Eye | Indigo | Pineal |
| 5 | Throat | Blue | Thyroid |
| 4 | Heart | Green | Thymus |
| 3 * | Solar Plexus | Yellow | Adrenals |
| 2 * | Navel, Sexual Spleen, Sacral Plexus | Orange | Pancreas |
| 1 | Root, Earth Base | Red | Gonads (Ovaries or testes) |

\*    The third and second chakras are sometimes interconnected (e.g.,
the second chakra can sometimes affect the adrenals, and the third
chakra can also influence the pancreas).

**The chakras, their names, colors, and associated glands.**

A person's major chakras should all rotate or circle in a
clockwise direction as you look at the person facing you.
These centers also shift and swirl while remaining fixed
more or less in the same location, much the same as the
human aura. (Think of the Northern Lights dancing in the
sky to get the right picture in your mind.)

Each major energy center has a different color indicating
different vibratory rates or frequencies. The colors in order
from lowest to highest frequency are red, orange, yellow,
green, blue, indigo (mid purple), and light purple.

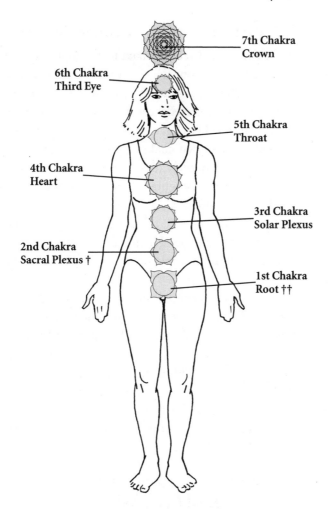

7th Chakra
Crown

6th Chakra
Third Eye

5th Chakra
Throat

4th Chakra
Heart

3rd Chakra
Solar Plexus

2nd Chakra
Sacral Plexus †

1st Chakra
Root ††

†    Also known as the Navel, Sexual, or Spleen Plexus
††   Also known as the Earth or Base Plexus.

**The location of the seven major chakras in relation to the human body.**

## The Seventh Chakra—Crown Chakra

The crown chakra is directly linked to the higher cosmic vibrations that come from the Creator or God. It is your connection to the God source, the Divine. Universal healing energy can be collected here and directed from this chakra through to other chakras, the auric field, and even into the body. The crown chakra is light purple in color and vibrates at an extremely high rate or frequency; of all the colors of these energy centers, light purple energy possesses the highest frequency.

From the top of the head, this center's energy expands upwards to a height of several inches (about seven to fourteen) above the head and just on the edge of the human auric field.

The crown chakra is connected to the pituitary gland (as explained in chapter 3). By performing the vowel intonation of M-A-Y in a specific way, certain gifts and benefits can be received.

In Buddhism and Hinduism, this is where enlightenment or joining with the Godhead can be attained. In Christianity, it is where Christ Consciousness resides. Finally, in mysticism, it is where Cosmic Consciousness occurs.

## The Sixth Chakra—Brow or Third Eye Chakra

The third eye chakra is the key to intuitive, creative, and psychic abilities. When working in harmony with the crown chakra, this energy center allows you to function more productively and fully in life.

The third eye chakra color is normally indigo (mid purple) and has a very high vibratory rate, just slightly below the light purple color of the crown chakra. It is located inside the middle of the head and expands outward to both the front and back. Medical intuitives, aura readers, and clairvoyants can see this special energy center as a circular swirl of purplish energy in front of the forehead. The swirl of energy should turn in a gentle clockwise motion when looking at the forehead.

The third eye or brow chakra, like the crown chakra, was also discussed in chapter 2. As explained there, this energy center is connected to the pineal gland inside the lower part of the brain. By chanting the vowel tone of THOH in a precise way, intuitive, creative, and psychic abilities can be developed or enhanced.

This energy center is important for the development of reading auras, seeing higher energy vibrations, and assimilating psychic impressions from a higher source.

## The Fifth Chakra—Throat Chakra

The throat chakra is the center for spoken intuitive knowledge and wisdom. If this energy center is opened properly, it can allow your intuitive counseling and teaching skills to manifest through spoken words of insight.

Gifted spiritual healers, teachers, and counselors use the energy of the throat chakra for helping others. The right words said at the appropriate time can help immensely in the healing process. The voice and the spoken word have true power.

The color of this energy center is blue. It has a high vibratory rate, just below the indigo and light purple colors.

On a physical level, the throat chakra is connected to the thyroid gland. This gland, which is a part of the endocrine glandular system, affects metabolism and releases certain hormones that influence the adrenals and nervous system.

If the throat chakra can be properly activated, the higher energy found in the chakra and in the aura can enter the throat, thyroid, and neck, maintaining a healthy essence in this area. An activated or "open" and balanced throat chakra will allow the wisdom of words to come forth. Physiologically, it will help the thyroid gland and parathyroids to function normally, aiding the endocrine glandular system of the body in keeping a proper balance. When "stimulated" in a certain manner, the thyroid gland can "speed up" in a person suffering from an underactive thyroid.

In the following pages, several techniques will be given to you for opening or activating the throat chakra, as well as a special stimulation exercise for the thyroid.

## Hand Chakra Opening Technique (Hand Warming Exercise)

There is an initial, preparatory technique that must be done prior to performing any of the throat chakra techniques.

Even though the hands, specifically the palm areas, are not considered major chakras or energy centers, they are still important. For a true healer to work more effectively, the palm (hand) chakras must be fully open.

In most individuals, these chakras are barely open. If you were to look at the palms of someone's hands and imagine a swirl of light or energy about the size of a quarter just hovering above the surface of the skin, then you would have an understanding of how small and partially opened most people's palm chakras are.

A gifted healer has the palm or hand energy centers completely open with the swirl of light or energy hovering above the whole hand including the thumbs and fingers. The healer's hands are very warm with nerve energy and natural healing essence flowing through both palms, both thumbs and all the fingers.

By having the palm energy centers properly open, a healer can send healing energy from his or her hands to the patient or client. The patient benefits greatly by receiving an increased amount of universal healing energy into his or her body, as well as being able to activate more of his or her own natural healing energy. In other words, with time, both the healer and the patient or client will become more effective as a healing team.

There are meridians of energy running from the chest, shoulders, and upper arms down the length of the arms and into the hands where they continue into both thumbs, both index fingers, and both middle fingers. These meridians end at the tips of the thumbs and index and middle fingers. It is from the tips of the thumbs and these fingers that specific nerve energy and healing energy can be released and directed to another person's body. These energies can also be released through the palms.

When the hand chakras are more open, the universal energy of the cosmic and the natural energy within an individual's own body will flow unimpeded down the meridians, through the palms, and finally out the thumbs and fingers. This helps to ensure that the individual or healer remains healthy, with the proper amount of universal

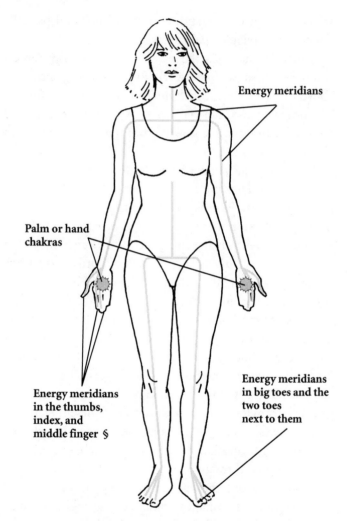

Energy meridians

Palm or hand
chakras

Energy meridians
in the thumbs,
index, and
middle finger §

Energy meridians
in big toes and the
two toes
next to them

§    Note that energy meridians are in the thumbs, index and middle
fingers (nerve energy also runs through these areas).

**The main energy meridians in the arms, hands, legs, and feet.
Palm chakras are also indicated here.**

energy and natural energy flowing through this part of the body and these meridians.

In order to "activate" and more fully open the palm chakras, the following special Hand Warming Exercise can be used.

First, find a comfortable chair to sit down in. Take a relaxing breath in and out and then put your hands together in a prayer position with fingers spread slightly apart. Now place your hands while still in this position, in your lap. Gently move the palms of each hand away from each other until there is a space of about four inches between the middle of each palm. Refer to the illustration on the following page.

Now, with your eyes either open or shut, start focusing all of your concentration upon your hands, especially the palms. Continue focusing here, feeling warmth and energy going into the hands. Keep this concentration for a few moments until you feel some warmth, some sensation, even a pulsation going into both palms. From this point, start to visualize a white fire or possibly a match being lit between your hands. Feel this white fire or lighted match on both palms, allowing the warmth to spread all over the surface of your skin. As the energy spreads across both palms, let it start to move up into your thumbs until you can feel a pulsation or warm sensation in your thumbs, particularly at the tips. Now let the warmth and energy that has increased in both palms move up your index fingers until you get a sensation in your finger tips that is similar to the sensation in your thumb tips. Finally, move the warmth and pulsing energy into both middle fingers.

Once this has been accomplished, focus all your attention on your hands, feeling the pulsing, warmth, and sensations

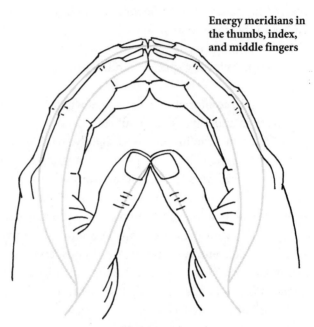

Energy meridians in
the thumbs, index,
and middle fingers

Space between
palms (about 4")

**Proper hand position for Hand Warming Exercise. Warmth
must be generated between palms in order to activate and
open the palm chakras.**

flowing completely through your hands, your palms, and
into your thumbs and respective fingers. Let this warming
sensation continue for a few more moments.

If you have trouble feeling the energy or warmth, try
imagining yourself outside on a hot summer day. Feel the
warmth of the sun beating down onto your hands, letting
the sun's rays hit the skin, then feel the heat penetrating

through the surface into the hands, completely warming both hands inside and out. You can also visualize or feel yourself placing your hands into a sink of very warm water. To help this, remember back to when you have washed dishes in hot water or you dipped your hands into hot bath water. Sometimes, the use of memory recall will help to trigger the desired effect.

Once you have succeeded at this Hand Warming Exercise, you will have begun to activate and open your palm (hand) chakras. The more you practice this Hand Chakra Opening Technique, the easier it will be for you to warm your hands, open the palm chakras properly and direct nerve energy, Universal Energy from above and natural healing energy from within into your hands and ultimately towards a client or patient.

Eventually, many of you will simply have to focus on your hands prior to performing your healing work, and the healing energy and warmth will go there automatically. The Palm Chakra Opening Technique will no longer be required! You will have increased your healing abilities.

## Thumb and Finger Technique

Once you have completed the Hand Warming Exercise, you are ready to try the Thumb and Finger Technique for activating or opening the throat chakra properly.

Take your right hand and move it from your lap upward to your throat area. Have you thumb, index, and middle fingers extended while the two remaining fingers of your right hand are closed. Place your right thumb gently onto the right side of your throat just beside the "voice box" (larynx) and put your right index and middle fingers onto

your throat just on the left side of the larynx directly opposite to where your thumb is positioned. For men, the
Adam's apple is the proper place; for women, the midpoint
between the base of the throat and chin is the desired location. Hold your thumb and two fingers here for three or
four minutes focusing on the warmth, energy, and pulsation at the tips of these areas. Soon, you will start to feel the
pulsing sensation moving into your throat, into your voice
box, and through to the back of your neck.

By holding your right thumb and two fingers here for a
small period of time, you enable the heat, nerve energy, and
natural healing energy to move into your throat. The heat
along with the energies will activate and "open" your throat
chakra and send a gentle, soothing energy into the thyroid
and parathyroids.

The heat in the hands, especially the palms, is important
for the activation of this chakra and any other chakra. The
warmth and the energies that go into the thyroid and surrounding areas will help to balance this gland and assist in
keeping the whole endocrine glandular system functioning
in harmony.

For those with an overactive thyroid condition, this simple yet important technique will help to slow down the thyroid in the same manner that a gentle massage will relax
the body. You will become less nervous and less agitated,
more relaxed and balanced. This thumb and finger technique may be repeated two or three more times over the
next week to ten days.

The unique exercise just described can also be used for
alleviating sore throats and for healing pain, stiffness, and
other problems in the neck area. It may even help neck

muscles to relax and lessen headaches. Remember that once you get the heat and natural energies moving into the throat, these sensations will continue to move through the neck, and even onto the scalp, sending healing essence into regions requiring help.

The Thumb and Finger Technique not only activates the throat chakra: it is also an important healing technique.

Once the throat chakra opens properly, you start to become more effective as a healer, teacher, communicator, and counselor and to access more of your true creative gifts.

## Throat Chakra Opening Technique (Palm Circling)

After using the Thumb and Finger Technique a few times, you can utilize the following exercise on a regular basis.

Once you have warmed both hands up using the Hand Warming Exercise, take both hands and move them from your lap upwards to the throat area. Keep your hands about six inches out and away from your throat, within your aura and the outer perimeter of your throat chakra. Now take your left hand away and put it down by your side or in your lap again.

Open your right hand with the palm facing towards your throat in the voice box area (midpoint of the throat). Keeping your hand about five or six inches away, slowly start to move your hand in a circular motion in front of the throat area, circling in a counterclockwise motion. Make slow, gentle circular motions in a small area that encompasses the complete throat from about the chin to the base of the throat. Continue this circular action with your hand and slowly move it an inch or two closer. You can perform this Palm Circling Technique with the palm facing towards you for a minute or two. This is all that is required to activate and allow the throat chakra to turn slowly and properly. If you focus on the throat area as you perform this technique, you will feel a slight sensation of movement with either a warm or cool presence to it. Always remember to turn your hand in a counterclockwise motion as you glance down at your palm. This will ensure that the chakra will turn the right way, "clockwise," as if someone was looking directly at you and your chakras.

You can practice the Palm Circling Technique whenever you feel that your throat chakra needs it. Chakras, if not used properly or often enough, will sometimes "close down" and need to be reactivated. This guarantees that this area of your body as well as your throat chakra will remain balanced and healthy.

Incidentally, the Palm Circling Technique, with the palm facing towards you, can be used for all the major energy centers or chakras. As we discuss the rest of the major chakras, we will again refer to this special technique.

## Thyroid Stimulation Technique

As mentioned earlier, there is a specific technique that can be performed in order to "speed up" the thyroid. This releases certain thyroid hormones necessary for good metabolism and for increased energy levels. For those suffering from an underactive thyroid gland, whether it is a small or large health concern, this stimulation exercise is excellent for temporary, if not eventual permanent relief.

There is two different ways of performing this technique. The first way involves the use of the Thumb and

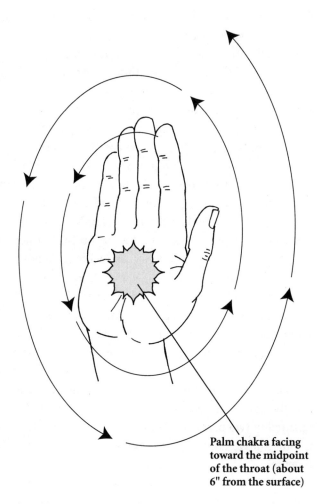

Palm chakra facing
toward the midpoint
of the throat (about
6" from the surface)

This is the way you should circle with your hand as you look
down toward it (palm facing toward you).

Fingers Technique along with the chanting of a specific sound in a very special way. The second method simply involves the toning or chanting of this sound by itself.

Starting with the first method is probably the best approach. Try the Thumb and Fingers Technique once more. This time as you lightly press your right thumb and two fingers against the appropriate parts of your throat, take in a deep breath and hold it for about five seconds, then release it slowly. Go back to normal breathing while focusing on your thyroid area. You are now ready to try the vowel intonation of K-A-Y-E-E. This particular toning sound is done in a lower note than the T-H-O-H or M-A-Y chants. The KAYEE chant is performed in a low to mid-C musical key. Once again, if you are not musically inclined, do not worry. As you practice toning K-A-Y-E-E, merely lower your voice a little into a slightly deeper sound than the M-A-Y chant.

Now, take another deep breath in, hold it for a few seconds, then open your mouth and chant K-A-Y first as you begin to release your breath, allowing the K-A-Y to come out as if you are singing. Then, slowly switch to Y-E-E in one fluid motion letting the Y-E-E sound continue until all your breath has been released slowly. Even though KAYEE is chanted in two parts, the toning exercises is performed in a nondisruptive way, letting both parts join smoothly together.

Try the KAYEE chant a second time, lowering or raising the musical key while paying attention to the vibration in your throat. Feel this vibration working completely through the whole throat as you tone KAYEE. By testing the musical scale, you will find the musical key or harmony that works best for you. The musical key of mid- to low C is only a guideline to assist you in finding the appropriate note that causes the proper vibration in your throat chakra. This vibration will trigger your thyroid gland to resonate or vibrate gently, causing it to "speed up," thereby releasing more thyroid hormones into your body. One of the results of this exercise is an increase of adrenaline or epinephrine.

The toning of the vowel chant K-a-y-e-e not only stimulates the thyroid and parathyroids, it activates the throat chakra to open more fully. If you simply wish to activate or open the throat chakra, the intonation of K-a-y-e-e once or twice will work effectively. If you have an underactive thyroid, toning with this important chant three to five times at one session will result in an increase of energy and stamina. This special technique has proved effective in the past for sufferers of underactive thyroids.

If you are one of these individuals who suffers from some form of this malady, performing the chant three to five times at one session and then chanting K-a-y-e-e three to five times once more in about two weeks will increase your vitality. After this point, you should only perform this technique about once a month, using three chants of K-a-y-e-e instead of five each time.

Avoid performing the Thyroid Stimulation Technique just before bedtime, as you will not be able to sleep afterwards. Your whole body will be activated with lots of energy, and you will be unable to achieve a restful state.

If you do not suffer from an underactive or overactive thyroid, and simply want to activate your throat chakra, chanting K-a-y-e-e once or twice is sufficient. You can repeat this technique about once a month if you feel the need.

This exercise can be used on certain mornings when you first wake up, especially if you are still tired and sluggish. Chant K-A-Y-E-E once or twice. You should start to notice your energy level increasing. This "wake up" exercise is more effective than several cups of coffee, but it should be used in moderation. Do not chant K-A-Y-E-E more than three times at a session!

You have now been given several methods to help you "open" your throat chakra, balance your endocrine glandular system, and remain healthier. When you can feel the energy in the throat chakra or in any of your seven major chakras, you become more aware of your body, your energy centers and, most importantly, your own healing energy. This awareness should allow you to remain healthy, happy and balanced and able to assist others in a profound way.

## The Fourth Chakra—The Heart Chakra

The heart chakra is the energy center that is important for the healing of self and others. The color radiating in this chakra is a beautiful light to mid green. This green energy is of a high vibratory rate and is a necessary color for true healing.

Individuals who operate from the heart are the healers, the caregivers, and comforters of society. All of you must learn to operate from this chakra, for this is where the spiritual path begins.

The Master Jesus performed most of his work and his healing using the love and compassion of an open heart chakra. In fact, many paintings and statues of Jesus Christ prominently display the heart of Jesus, known as the Sacred Heart.

The heart in you is the heart in all.
—Ralph Waldo Emerson
(philosopher and essayist,
1803–82)

The heart energy center with its high vibration of healing essence is associated on a physical level with the thymus gland in the upper chest. This gland, which is located about two inches above the heart, is largely responsible for the balance of the body's immune system. In its capacity as *the heart of the body's defense mechanisms*, the thymus gland initiates a large number of specialized cells that help fight infections. These specialized cells are called T-cells.

If the heart chakra is open properly, allowing love and healing into this center, the thymus gland will receive the green healing energy in a lower vibratory form as the chakra energy "steps down" from the auric field and chakra center into the physical form. This healing vibration will trigger the thymus gland to resonate slightly, releasing the T-cells and other secretions that are necessary for the immune system. The thymus, which is part of the endocrine glandular system, becomes balanced and in harmony.

A major problem in our fast-paced world is stress. Stress can affect the thymus gland, causing it to become unbalanced and unhealthy. This leads to disease! Reducing stress and opening the heart chakra for love is important for everyone.

## Heart Chakra Opening Technique

There are several special techniques that can be used to awaken and open the heart chakra. The first technique you will learn to do is referred to as the Heart Chakra Opening Technique.

Initially, start with the Hand Warming Exercise. Once you have warmed your hands up, particularly your palms, place your right hand on the chest in the center partially over the heart. With your eyes, either open or shut, begin to focus on your hand as it rests here. Feel the warmth of the palm upon the surface of the skin. Keep focusing all your attention on the slight warmth or energy here, letting the warmth start to spread from the hand onto the surface of your skin directly underneath. Allow the warmth or energy to continue expanding from a small area of the surface to a larger area that is about the size of the whole hand. As you continue concentrating, you will soon feel the warmth or sensation completely beneath your hand, including your thumb and fingers. At this point, feel the warmth or energy spreading about an inch or two beyond the perimeter of your hand. Continue concentrating on the warmth here in your chest area directly below the hand for a few more seconds.

For those of you who have difficulty sensing warmth in your palms and hands, do not be concerned. If you feel coolness in your palms or merely an awareness of your hands over the chest, that is acceptable when you first experiment with this technique. Allow the coolness or awareness of your hand to spread across the surface of your chest in the same manner. Whether you experience warmth, a coolness, or only an awareness of the hand upon the chest, the technique will still work; the heart chakra will become "activated." You may or may not be aware of this, nevertheless, the process will have begun. Any warmth, sensation, or concentration upon the heart energy center will activate or energize this center to open up.

For those of you who experience the warmth spreading across the chest just beneath the hand, you are actually feeling the heart center activating and "opening up." This is a major step in healing yourself and, eventually, in healing other people.

Most human beings in our materialistic world have their heart chakras closed down during their adult lifetime. More people should experience an open heart chakra in order for a more enlightened society to evolve.

## Breath Focusing Technique

The next technique for you to attempt is a special breathing exercise that can be done at the end of the Heart Chakra Opening Technique. It is a natural progression to combine the breathing exercise with concentration.

Once you have finished focusing on the warmth or energy in the chest area, leave your right hand in this same position and begin to take nice, deep breaths into your lungs. After filling your lungs, release your breath slowly through your nose. Feel the breath going in and out of your chest. Pay attention to the chest rising and falling with each breath. All your concentration should be upon your breath and your chest. Notice your hand as it rests on your chest, rising and falling with each deep breath. This helps to ensure that you are doing chest breathing exercises and not diaphragmatic breathing (diaphragmatic breathing will be used later).

After four to five slow, deep breaths in and out, return to normal breathing still concentrating on your chest. The breathing exercise is important because it draws vital life force, *chi,* into your lungs and physical being. This assists greatly in the opening of the heart energy center.

It is now time to move on to the next special heart chakra techniques.

## The Baby Technique

This is a unique technique that can be used to release deep buried pain and emotions, as well as to release the true healing energy of love. This is an effective emotional release and love release exercise for all people, though women may find this especially helpful.

As you focus on your normal breathing, with your right hand resting on your chest, start to imagine yourself looking at a beautiful child in a crib. This visualization may trigger a happy memory for some. As you look at the baby, feel the love in your heart for this precious child. In your mind, reach down and pick the baby up, holding him or her close to your breast. As you hold this baby in your arms, the baby whom you love very much, feel the warmth of his or her body next to you. Hear the baby making little noises. Give the child a little hug and feel the love and warmth in your chest starting to expand. Gently rock this beautiful child back and forth, then give him or her a tender kiss on the forehead. Feel the love and joy in your heart continuing to spread across your chest. Finally, as you feel the love, the warmth, or perhaps a slight sadness inside, place the baby back into the crib and smile down at the little one.

Let the love and warmth in your heart be directed towards him or her. Feel the love pouring forth from the heart center towards this child of God. Do this for a few more seconds, then take a deep breath in and slowly release it. At the same time, stop visualizing the baby. Let yourself come back to full awareness of where you are.

## The Loved One Technique

The following technique can be performed as a continuation of the previous one. After you have finished with the Baby Technique, change the picture in your mind into an image of someone you love very much. Allow yourself to keep the feeling of warmth and love in your chest from the previous exercise. Focus on this person, seeing his or her face looking and smiling at you. This special individual may even be someone you loved in the past, such as a parent or grandparent who has passed on.

Now, imagine yourself walking towards him or her with your arms open wide and then wrap your arms around this person as you come into contact with each other. Hold this loved one in your arms and feel all the love in your heart for that person. Let the emotion come forth. You can even tell this special person that you love him or her. Feel the warmth, emotion, or sensation in your heart continuing to spread all the way across the chest. Finally, direct the love or warmth in your heart chakra out to this being. Give him or her a final hug and then release your hold and say "I love you. Goodbye."

Once again feel your attention returning to the place where you are sitting or lying.

Some of you may wish to use a son, a daughter, a spouse, or even a close friend in this visualization. If you decide to use the vision of a relative or close friend who has died as your special loved one, realize that remembering a dear departed person may solicit emotions of sadness, pain, or perhaps guilt. This is a way of forcing buried emotions to the surface where you are able to release them in a positive, healing manner. You can also transcend the grave in order to express your feelings and thoughts to a loved one who is in the higher planes of heaven. This can be a powerful healing tool for many.

People who have difficulty with the Baby Technique may use the Loved One Technique. In many situations, this technique may be more effective for both men and women than the Baby Technique.

Both of these special visualization exercises may be done together with the Baby Technique being completed first and the Loved One Technique following in a smooth sequence.

If you simply wish to use just one of these techniques, experiment with both, then use the technique that is most effective for you. The more you practice with one or both visualization exercises, the easier and quicker it will be for you to open your heart chakra.

Eventually, you will be able to focus on your heart center without doing these exercises, opening and closing this chakra at will. This takes training and persistence for some people. In other cases, individuals who are natural "feelers" will achieve this proficiency very quickly.

These two heart chakra emotional release techniques can result in different experiences for different people. Perhaps you will feel tremendous warmth and love in your chest area, or you may feel intense sadness and start to cry. A few of you will experience a tightness, pressure, or pain in the vicinity of the heart. Some of you might even think that you are having heart problems or, in rare circumstances, a mild bout with anxiety.

These are some of the results of doing these techniques and activating and opening the heart chakra. These results are signs of true emotional and physical healing within. These varied feelings will soon dissipate as you return to normal consciousness and focus on your surroundings.

Both the Baby Technique and the Loved One Technique can be attempted again in a few days or even a week later. The next time you experiment with either or both exercises, you will be acutely aware of the heart center starting to warm up and open more easily. Most of you will feel a very pleasant sensation spreading across the chest as the heart chakra opens up and allows healing and love energy to flow naturally.

If you experienced sadness, heart palpitations, pain, or pressure in the chest or mild anxiety the first time, the second and third attempts will be less unpleasant. You will soon start to enjoy the warm, loving energy moving through your heart center and through your whole chest as it replaces the unpleasantness. In essence, you have cleared an energy block, released deeply buried pain and started to heal on an emotional, physical, and mental level. You have even touched your soul, your true being within.

The ultimate goal of performing all these techniques is to teach you how to quickly focus your attention on your heart chakra and open it at will. Eventually, as you develop mastery over the heart chakra, you will no longer need to perform the Heart Chakra Opening Technique, the Breath Focusing Technique, the Baby Technique, and the Loved

One Technique—but please use any or all of these techniques if you feel the need. For example, if you have had a trying day or week, the Baby Technique can be effective in releasing any emotional pain you have received from others during that difficult period.

You should always do some deep breathing exercises whenever you focus on and open up your heart center. This holds true whether you are proficient at doing energy work or are a novice.

## The Puppy or Kitten Technique

You can use either a puppy or a kitten to focus on as you do this particular meditation technique. (A puppy will be used in the following description of this heart center exercise, but you can substitute a kitten if you prefer.)

This technique can be performed immediately following the Heart Chakra Opening and Breath Focusing Techniques. This is a smooth, simple progression after performing these techniques.

While you still have your right hand resting upon your chest, feeling the warmth within and still fully aware of your breath, return to normal breathing and begin to focus on a cute little puppy sitting on the grass next to your bare feet. Picture yourself standing outside on a warm, pleasant day.

In your mind, see yourself reaching down and picking up the cute, furry puppy up in your arms. Bring it to your chest, then give the little animal a gentle hug. Imagine the warmth of its body next to your chest as you hold him in your arms. Feel the love in your heart for this furry little puppy.

Start to rub the puppy's head and body with one hand as you continue to hold it in your arms. Feel the warmth and pressure of the animal against your chest. Keep rubbing its furry little head and body as it nuzzles its cold nose up against your neck. Even imagine the little animal trying to lick your ear as you hold it. Give the puppy a final gentle squeeze and feel the love in your heart for the little one.

Now put the puppy down by your feet and watch as it starts to run through the green grass. The furry little creature is clumsy and keeps falling down. You laugh as you watch it running, falling, and playing in the grass. Feel the laughter, joy, and happiness within your heart center as you continue to watch the puppy playing.

Finally, take a deep breath in, hold it for about three seconds, and then release it slowly through your nose. Allow yourself to return to conscious awareness, keeping the pleasant sensation in your chest area.

The Puppy Technique may also be used by itself. For instance, if you are feeling sad and unhappy for whatever reason (or perhaps after trying the Baby or Loved One Technique you experienced some of the unpleasant emotions that are sometimes associated with these two exercises), the Puppy Technique is a wonderful visualization exercise for changing unpleasant feelings into warm, pleasant ones. This technique helps to initiate joyful memories and happy emotions.

## Warmth Opening Flower Technique

The following technique can be used for the solar, sacral, and base chakras as well as for the heart chakra.

This exercise should be preceded by the Heart Chakra Opening and Breath Focusing Techniques. Remember how you placed your right hand over your chest and felt the warmth of your palm going into the heart center, then focused on your breath going in and out of your lungs.

After you have performed these two techniques together, begin the Warmth Opening Flower Technique.

Focus your attention inside your chest just an inch or two below the surface where your hand is resting. Picture a beautiful green flower residing there. The flower is all closed up. Now, as you continue sitting or lying there in a comfortable position, think of yourself sitting outside on a warm summer day. You are lying on the side of a hill enjoying the warmth of the sun. Feel the warmth, the energy of the sun penetrating your whole body, then feel the intense warmth of the sun moving down through your body from the top of your head into your toes. From your toes, feel the energy, the sun's energy, moving all the way up again until it gets to your chest area. In some instances, if you can remember a time when you were tanning yourself, you may trigger this feeling of warmth.

As you concentrate on your chest, feeling both the warmth of the sun and the warmth of your hand resting there, let this energy move inside until it reaches the beautiful, green flower that is still closed up. As it does, see and feel the green flower opening up with its flower petals starting to unfurl. In your mind, watch and feel these lovely green petals spreading slowly across your chest, into your heart, through your lungs, across your ribs, and completely through your whole chest cavity. Feel the energy of your hand and the sun pouring through these green flower petals and spreading across your chest. Finally, feel and see the flower petals fully opened, fully expanded. These petals along with the sun's energy and the hand's warmth are all the way across the chest, even up to the shoulders, neck, and upper arms.

Enjoy the sensations as you are lying there, outside on a warm summer day. Feel the pleasant warmth of the sun continuing to penetrate into the heart chakra and spread throughout the whole chest. You are relaxed and peaceful, allowing the energy to pour through the heart, the lungs, the ribcage, and the thymus gland in the upper part of the chest. Feel the warmth and pleasant sensation for a few minutes more. Let this wonderful, soothing energy flow through your chest. Enjoy the loving, peaceful, and contented feeling within.

After three or four minutes of focusing on the wonderful, warm energy in this area of your body, visualize the sun setting as you are still lying outside. As the sun sets, the beautiful green flower petals are starting to shrink and close up within your chest. Slowly, feel and see these petals getting smaller and smaller until they are just opened slightly underneath the palm of your hand. Feel the warmth about the diameter of your palm inside your chest. You are allowing your heart center to remain open enough for the healing energy to flow through this area.

Now, take a deep breath in, hold it for a few seconds, and release it slowly through your nose or mouth. Return to normal breathing and normal awareness. You should feel relaxed and still experience a slight warmth in the heart chakra.

This simple yet effective technique allows you to learn to open and close your heart center at will. For that matter, you will also be able to use a slightly altered version of this technique to open and close other energy centers as well.

The more you practice the Warmth Opening Flower Technique, the easier it will become for you. Eventually, you will no longer need to perform this exercise as you become proficient at opening and closing your heart chakra. At this point, you will need only focus on your heart chakra in order to open and close it at will.

If you can learn to do this effectively, you will become a better healer, counselor, and teacher. You will start directing healing energy throughout your body and keep yourself healthy on a physical, mental, and emotional level. Diseases such as breast cancer, lung cancer, and heart disorders are less likely to occur because of the love and healing energy moving properly through this area of your body.

In many circumstances, if an illness is not advanced, the release of healing energy through the heart chakra will help to heal the body. For example, people who have irregular heartbeats have been known to heal the problem by working with the healing energy of the heart center.

## Hand Circling Technique

The Palm Circling Technique in the discussion of the throat chakra (pp. 109–11) can also be used to balance the heart chakra. Place the palm of your right hand in front of your heart energy center about three to four inches away from your body and perform the same circling exercise.

When you open the heart chakra, you will become kinder, gentler, and more loving towards yourself and others. You will learn how to touch the hearts and souls of many, creating a better world.

# The Third Chakra—
# The Solar Plexus Chakra

The solar plexus chakra, which is located about one to three inches directly above the navel, has a lower vibratory rate than the heart chakra. The color associated with this major energy center is yellow.

This chakra is attuned to the lower, base emotions of the physical world. Most individuals operate from this energy center and the two lower ones, the sacral plexus and base chakras.

The adrenals, which are part of the endocrine glandular system and are located on top of each of the kidneys, are connected to the solar plexus chakra. The sympathetic nervous system is the bridge between the higher chakra energy of the solar plexus and the adrenals.

On a psychic and spiritual level, this chakra is connected with the empathic skills and sensitivity to human emotions. Many gifted empaths and sensitives are finely attuned to others through this energy center; some people consider their empathic ability a curse rather than a gift. In reality, if this ability is fully developed and used properly, it is a blessed gift.

An area of the adrenals, called the cortex, is sometimes referred to as "the mirror of our emotions." This is a very apt name because many hormonal secretions that directly influence how we feel are produced here.

On a physical level, the adrenals create the "fight or flight" response in human beings. These two endocrine glands or organs contain the inner medulla and outer cortex. The inner medulla produces epinephrine and norepinephrine. These hormones stimulate the heart and increase blood sugar, muscular strength, and endurance. They also contract blood vessels, stop bleeding, and transmit nerve impulses. Epinephrine is also commonly called adrenaline.

The outer cortex of the adrenals creates a type of sex hormone along with other steroid hormones. These secretions have a tendency to make you feel good, happy, and balanced.

If you can learn to open the solar plexus chakra, you can release some of these beneficial secretions that give you a sense of peace, well-being, and contentment. You can also release and direct healing energy from this chakra. This energy will flow through the stomach, intestinal tract, muscles, and internal parts that are also associated with the solar plexus. This pleasant healing essence can soothe an upset stomach, ease pain in the intestinal tract, and generally relax and calm all internal organs in this area.

If you suffer from irritable bowel syndrome, Crohn's disease, or any other bowel malady, opening the solar plexus energy center allows for healing and can greatly reduce pain and discomfort. If you suffer from a low sex drive, learning to open and close this major energy center can help to correct the problem.

Pent-up anger and emotions can also be released in a healthy way as you work with the energy of the solar plexus chakra. When you work with your solar plexus center or other major energy centers, you develop a sense of well-being and balance.

## Solar Plexus Opening Technique

In order to activate and open the solar plexus chakra, you will use three of the techniques used for opening and activating the heart chakra. The exercises to use are the Heart (aka Solar) Chakra Opening, the Breath Focusing, and the Warmth Opening Flower Techniques. Please review these techniques if you need to; however, these three techniques will be altered slightly in the following descriptions. Remember as you do these exercises that they should be done together in a smooth, easy progression.

Once you have done the Hand Warming Exercise already described (page 102 and following), place your right hand lightly on your stomach, about two to three inches above your navel. Feel and experience the warmth in the solar plexus just beneath the palm of your hand in the same way that you did when you focused on the heart chakra.

Allow the sensation to spread across your solar plexus and into your internal organs here. Once the energy or warmth has spread fully across, start the Breath Focusing Technique. Only this time, do deep diaphragmatic breathing instead of chest breathing. Let your breath go deep into your lower chest and diaphragm, hold it there for a few seconds, and then exhale slowly through your nose. Feel your hand rising and falling gently as it rests on your stomach area. Continue deep breathing two or three more times and then return to normal breathing.

Now, focus on the warmth of your hand upon the solar plexus. Imagine yourself outside once more on a beautiful summer day. Feel the sun's warmth along with the warmth of your palm penetrating inside, about two inches below the skin. This time, imagine a yellow flower all folded up starting to open as the energy touches it. Do the same thing with this yellow flower in the solar plexus as you did with the green flower of the heart chakra. Let the beautiful yellow flower petals fully open and expand throughout the internal organs and across the solar area. In your mind, leave this flower fully opened with its warm sensation for up to about five minutes if you want.

Experience the peaceful, easy feeling as you are lying outside on a beautiful warm day. Feel the sun penetrating through your stomach area and relaxing your whole being. Enjoy the moment as you lie there at peace. Finally, see the sun starting to set once more. As it does, the yellow flower petals slowly contract until the flower is barely open underneath the palm of your hand. The warmth below your hand should now be about the diameter of your palm. This allows you to keep the energy center slightly open for proper balance and health.

Some people may feel pressure or uncomfortable sensations in the solar plexus chakra when these three combined techniques are tried for the first time. This feeling merely indicates that there is a physical, emotional, or energy block here. Stress, worry, anxiety, and nervousness can sometimes cause blocks of this kind.

Individuals who store everything in their "gut" will feel this pressure or sensation as the chakra energy starts to force its way through the solar plexus and internal organs. This is a sign that healing energy is starting to flow to where it is needed.

Performing these three techniques a second or even a third time will lessen the uncomfortable sensation and slowly change it to a warm, contented sensation. Some sadness, anger, or pain will probably be released in a beneficial healing manner.

Eventually, you will be able to open and close the solar plexus center easily and quickly, with no unpleasant side effects.

As with the heart chakra, you will become an expert at opening and closing the solar plexus chakra at will or when needed. For those of you who are natural feelers, these techniques will produce wonderful results in a very short time; for example, you may become very relaxed or sleepy after performing this exercise.

## Hand Circling Technique

As per the illustration on page 111 in the section of this chapter on the throat chakra, you can use the Hand Circling Technique to balance the solar plexus chakra and allow it to turn in a natural way. Place your right hand in front of your solar area, about four inches away from the surface, and perform the circling exercise.

For relaxation, anger release, and stress reduction, the opening of the solar center is important.

## The Second Chakra— Sacral Plexus or Sexual Chakra

The sacral plexus chakra is located about one to three inches below the navel. The color associated with this major energy center is orange and has a lower rate of vibration than the solar plexus chakra. The sacral energy center is connected to power, control (to a small extent), and sexual energy. The desire to reproduce our own kind is entrenched in this center. Attraction towards other individuals and the sense of self-protection originates from here to a certain degree.

On a physical level, this energy center is connected to the pancreas. This organ is part of the endocrine glandular system, and is located in the abdomen. It releases certain digestive enzymes which, when properly balanced, can slow the human aging process.

This important energy center is sometimes referred to as the sexual chakra because the opening of this chakra initiates the release of sexual hormones into the body by the stimulation of the gonads and other glands of the endocrine glandular system. People who have their sacral or sexual chakra "too wide open" are sexually overactive; nymphomaniacs and individuals addicted to sex are prime examples. People who have little or no sex drive are suffering from just the opposite phenomena of this disorder; their sexual chakra is closed. The glands involved in producing sexual hormones in this area are underactive.

Either extreme is not healthy. As a human being, you are sexual and sexuality is a part of your make-up. The release of proper amounts of sexual hormones can make you feel alive, happy, and contented. Insufficient release of certain secretions will speed up the aging process and create a feeling of unhappiness and discontent within. Overactive hormones will keep you trapped in the lower, baser emotions; lust, not love, will rule your life. You will never attain true enlightenment or spiritual awakening at this lower level. A proper balance between both extremes must be found. The opening and balancing of the sacral plexus chakra will result in inner contentment, better personal relationships, and a healthy and balanced digestive system.

## Sacral Plexus Opening Techniques

You will be using the same three opening techniques explained in the solar plexus section of this chapter. To reiterate, you will use the Heart Chakra Opening, the Breath Focusing, and the Warmth Opening Flower Techniques. Once again, these special techniques will be slightly varied as you focus on the sacral energy center.

This time, after you have warmed up your hands properly, place your right hand onto the sacral plexus center an inch or two below the navel in the middle of this area.

Use the Heart Chakra Opening Technique to allow the warmth or sensation in your palm to work through the area of the sacral plexus directly beneath your right hand.

Once more, focus on your breathing, feeling the breath go deep into the lungs and diaphragm. Try to sense the air going down into the sacral center. After two or three deep diaphragmatic breaths, return to normal breathing.

Now, as before, imagine yourself outside on a beautiful warm day. This time, as you picture the sun and feel it shining onto your body, move the sun's energy into the sacral plexus area and experience this warmth and the warmth of your palm penetrating into the sacral plexus. Allow it to penetrate inside to a depth of two or three inches, where a lovely orange flower resides. The flower's petals are all closed.

The energies from your hand and from the sun strike the orange flower causing the orange petals to slowly open up. Let these petals, along with the warmth, expand completely across this area and also into your internal organs here. Feel and experience the orange petals and the soothing sensations spreading from hip to hip and deep within. Allow this pleasant energy to spread right through your lower back. As you lie here under the rays of the summer sun, enjoy the warmth, pleasant sensations, and peace within the sacral plexus center. Fully experience this meditation for several minutes, then see the sun setting again. As the sun sets below the horizon, feel and see these orange petals slowly contracting until the flower is just open to the size of the palm of your hand. This will ensure that this important energy center remains open enough for you to receive the right amount of healing energy.

The Warmth Opening Flower Technique will also let some of the warmth and energy trickle down from the sacral plexus chakra into the base chakra, initiating an awakening there. The Hand Circling Technique should be used on the sacral plexus chakra as well.

## The First Chakra— The Base, Root, or Earth Chakra

Of all the seven major chakras, the base chakra is of the lowest vibratory rate and is associated with the color red. It is connected through the feet chakras with the energy of Mother Earth. Your deepest survival instincts and primordial urges come from this center. The basest, most primitive emotions reside here, including an intense desire to procreate. Even though the energy vibrations are lower and not spiritual in nature like the higher chakras, the base chakra is of prime importance for health, vitality, and for maintaining a true balance for you as a physical and spiritual being.

A deep reverence for the earth, nature, and all living creatures can be found through this energy center.

The base or root chakra is very closely linked with the serpent power, *chi*, or kundalini energy that resides near the base of the spine. This powerful energy will be discussed in great detail in the following chapter.

## Base Chakra Opening Technique

Because the energy flowing down from the sacral chakra will start to warm up and activate the base (root) chakra in most people, the three basic opening techniques that you used for the heart, solar, and sacral energy centers are not necessary here. Just lie or sit in a comfortable, relaxed position and take a few initial deep breaths. This is all that is required to prepare for the following Base Chakra Opening Technique. All the other techniques that were used on your other major energy centers have already initiated the awakening and opening of this first chakra.

To begin, focus all your attention on your base and picture a red flower curled up within. Now, as you continue to concentrate on this area, feel a pressure, a sensation, or a warmth here. Then imagine yourself outside on a warm summer day. Experience the sun's energy penetrating through your groin area and striking the red flower. The warmth of the sun lets the flower petals open up and spread through your base chakra. Feel the warmth spreading as the red flower petals continue to expand. Finally, see and feel these red petals fully expanded from one side of the body to the other side. Even feel and visualize the flowers and warmth in the upper thighs.

Enjoy the warmth and pleasant sensations for up to about five minutes. Then see the sun setting. As it sets, the red petal start to slowly shrink until they are just open to about the diameter of a three-inch circle. Let the slight warmth or sensation remain here to allow the healing energy to flow through this area.

In rare circumstances, there may be a few who will experience some uncomfortable sensations in the base chakra the first time. Just repeat the Base Chakra Opening Technique a few more times. Soon, the unpleasant sensations will be replaced by a warm, pleasant feeling. The unpleasant sensation indicates a physical, emotional, or energy block. The proper opening of the base energy center will help alleviate any or all of these problems.

You have now learned how to properly activate and open the major chakras of your body. Eventually, you should become a master at working with your own energy centers. This helps to ensure that you will be more balanced, healthier, happier, and contented, as well as attaining rapid growth on your special path to enlightenment.

All of us are eternal souls with a physical body. The use of chakra energy creates a special connection with the true self within and with the soul. It is the evolution of your soul, your light being within, that really results from the activation of the human chakra system.

The divine spark of the Creator resides in all of you and needs to be shown in this earthly world that you call home for now.

> No labor, according to Diogenes, is good but that which aims at producing courage and strength of soul rather than of body.
> —Epictetus (Greek philosopher, first century C.E.)

# Chapter 7

# *Kundalini and Chakra Energy for Healing and Enlightenment*

> Once we open up to the flow of energy within our body, we also open up to the flow of the energy in the universe.
> —Wilhelm Reich (psychoanalyst and theorist, 1897–1957)

Within all of us is an incredible energy that can be tapped and released for wondrous results. As mentioned briefly in chapter 6, this energy is called kundalini. It is also referred to as *chi*, *prana*, serpent power, or the life force.

This natural energy or *chi* resides at the base of the spinal column, just between the anus and reproductive organs.

Kundalini is an ancient Sanskrit word that comes from the root term *kundala* meaning "coiled." In Hindu mythology, there was a goddess known as "Kundalini." She was full of sexual energy and appeared in the form of a sleeping serpent wrapped around the base of the spine.

Through proper arousal techniques, the kundalini energy can flow up the spinal column via the sympathetic nervous division (part of the autonomic system) and then out through the top of the skull where the crown chakra is located.

When this powerful energy is "awakened" or aroused in the base chakra, it can be also directed in and through the six other major chakras. As this energy flows here, it too will work through the endocrine glandular system of the human body.

In essence, the seven major energy centers or chakras are connected to the endocrine glandular system via the sympathetic nervous division of the autonomic nervous system.

The extremely high vibratory rates of chakra energy will work in harmony or "sympathy" with the sympathetic system. This special nervous system or division is attuned to the cosmic vibrations, universal energy, the human aura, and virtually all spiritual energies that originate from the Creator and the heavenly fields above. (It is unfortunate that medical science does not recognize the true potential of this harmonious system, but in time they will.)

Both the endocrine glandular system and the sympathetic nervous system (division) will be discussed in this chapter.

Certain techniques for releasing and working with the kundalini energy will be given to you as well. If these techniques are done properly, a safe and beneficial release of this wonderful natural energy will be the result.

You should also be aware that in some instances dancing, singing, walking, and running can stimulate the life force, allowing it to flow gently up the spine, through the chakras, and out the top of the head or crown chakra. Even listening to beautiful music sometimes causes a rush of this energy to flow up the spine, giving you a sense of elation. As children playing, you would have released kundalini flow and experienced high energy levels and happiness.

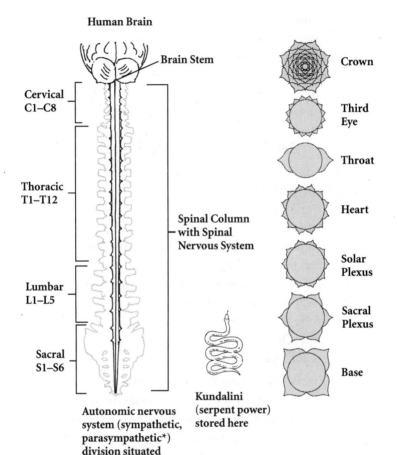

Human Brain

Brain Stem

Cervical
C1–C8

Thoracic
T1–T12

Spinal Column
with Spinal
Nervous System

Lumbar
L1–L5

Sacral
S1–S6

Autonomic nervous
system (sympathetic,
parasympathetic*)
division situated
along both sides of
spinal column

Kundalini
(serpent power)
stored here

Crown

Third
Eye

Throat

Heart

Solar
Plexus

Sacral
Plexus

Base

\* The parasympathetic division is associated with automatic
breathing and the heartbeat.

**Illustration showing the interrelationship of the chakra
system, spinal nervous system, sympathetic nervous division,
and kundalini.**

The illustration on page 139 is provided in order to show you how the seven major chakras, kundalini, the spinal or central nervous system, and the autonomic nervous system with its sympathetic and parasympathetic divisions are wholly related. These systems and divisions will be discussed throughout the remainder of this chapter.

## Benefits of Kundalini Energy

Before discussing the techniques or exercises that can be used for awakening and releasing this potent energy, an understanding of the benefits of working with kundalini and chakra energy should be known.

The following list covers many of the benefits associated with the proper release of both kundalini and chakra energy. The high vibrations of each of the major chakras are closely attuned with the serpent power residing at the base of the spine. Kundalini flow can trigger the chakras to open and release wonderful energy into each of the seven chakras and into the body.

- Stress Reduction. This energy greatly reduces anxiety and stress in both mind and body. Certain chemicals are released into the bloodstream to calm the emotions. This energy can often work on the nerves the same as a gentle, soothing massage.

- Spiritual Growth. Every time you work with this energy within, you develop more spiritual insight and more spirituality.

- Psychic Development. Kundalini flow increases your psychic abilities. This energy can help to open the crown and third eye chakras more fully, resulting in the use of more of your psychic nature.

- Increased Sexual Pleasure. With training and practice, a release of sexual energy, which is closely connected to kundalini, can be achieved. Thus, you experience "energy sex" along with the normal physical pleasure and orgasm.

- Heightened Self-Awareness. With the release of kundalini and chakra energy, you become more aware of the true you, the higher self within. You develop the knowledge that you are an eternal soul residing in a temporary physical form.

- Attainment of Mystical Union—Cosmic Consciousness. Proper use of kundalini flow allows the crown chakra and the eighth chakra (located about eighteen inches directly above the crown) to connect and then lets the God energy or Universal Energy from above enter through your chakras into your body and whole being. Divine illumination or "at-one-ment" is the wondrous result.

- Increased Stamina. The release of the *prana* on a daily basis helps to increase your vitality and energy level. More stamina is the result.

- Promotion of Healing Process. The continued use of both kundalini and chakra energy helps to heal the physical body and mind. Pain is decreased and cells rejuvenate through energy work.

- Slowing Down of Aging Process. The release of kundalini into the body via the sympathetic nervous system affects the hormonal secretions of the endocrine glandular system in such a way as to balance the glands and slow the aging process. In certain situations, a gradual reversal of the effects of aging may be experienced.

- Expansion and Cleansing of the Human Aura. The flow of this powerful energy will expand and cleanse your auric field. This ensures that negative emanations or colors are dispersed from your aura before they can affect you on a physical level. A strong, expanded aura will help to maintain your health and affect others in a loving, peaceful manner.

- Balanced and Opened Chakras. As mentioned, the release of kundalini energy will trigger each of the major chakras to open and release high energy into the part of the body where each chakra resides. Thus, healing energy will flow into areas where it is needed the most.

- Balanced Endocrine Glandular System. Kundalini energy flow will affect the major chakras, which in turn affects the endocrine glands in a positive, beneficial way. Chemical imbalances can be reversed and the release of certain secretions can result in a sense of contentment within yourself.

- Increased Mental Acuity. Kundalini energy, when released in the brain where both the third

eye and crown chakras are located, will affect
the brain and these chakras in a profound way.
You will start to use more of your brain capacity
and your psychic abilities.

In essence, kundalini—your energy within, can be used for
healing and the raising of human consciousness.

## Kundalini Arousal and Flow Techniques

There are special methods that can be used to arouse or
activate the kundalini within and then send it through the
body in a safe, effective manner.

Be warned, however: this *prana* or life force that sleeps at
the base of the spine is very powerful. If released in an
uncontrolled manner, an overpowering surge of energy can
erupt.

Controlled methods such as meditation, yoga exercises,
and visualization techniques can be used to arouse and
direct this potent energy in a positive way that is gentle and
soothing. This energy is also a powerful healing force for
both the mind and body.

Before discussing the special kundalini energy techniques, a final word of caution should be given. An individual who is unstable or ill prepared to work with kundalini
and chakra energy can inadvertently or improperly release
this energy within the body, precipitating some very
unpleasant side effects. As well, a person ill trained in
working with these high vibrational energies can cause
emotional and physical upheavals in their subjects or
clients.

Some of these side effects are anxiety or panic attacks, physical pain in parts of the body associated with certain major chakras, sadness, depression, nervousness, sleeplessness, and irritability. In certain situations, kundalini energy can erupt like a volcano, pouring out of the crown chakra in a powerful, violent manner. Cellular damage in parts of the body may result. Kundalini should therefore be treated with the respect it deserves.

The good news is there are proper and safe ways of preparing to work with kundalini energy. The techniques discussed in chapters 2 and 3 on the crown and third eye chakras were two of the steps necessary to prepare you to work with the *prana* or serpent power within yourself; chapter 6 covered the rest of the techniques needed to assist you in doing energy work properly and safely.

Many teaching systems devoted to kundalini and chakra energy work place their emphasis on the earth energy, the chakras of the feet and particularly the base or root chakra as starting points. These systems or schools of thought believe that earth energy or "Mother Earth" and the base chakra are most important. They believe that the energy of the earth should be brought up through the feet chakras into the base chakra or, if sitting in a proper position, the earth energy should go into the base center directly. The base or root chakras should then be activated and opened causing kundalini stored nearby to arouse and then flow up the spine, through the other six major chakras, finally exiting out the top of the head (crown chakra).

For most individuals starting out on this path (and for many others who have inactive or blocked energy centers), this method is harsh and difficult, or it may be ineffective altogether. Even though the energy of the earth is important and the base chakra should be activated, there are other aspects to consider.

As human beings, we need the Universal Energy or Spirit Energy from the Creator, as well as the energy of Mother Earth. Lastly, your own internal energy, the chakra energy and life force within, must be associated with both the energy of the earth below and the energy of the Creator from above. All three energies are essential for health, balance, and harmony.

This Spirit or Universal Energy is present in the world all about you. It must be used before starting any other kundalini practices, in order to open the chakras properly and effectively. This ensures that the kundalini energy within will activate safely and then flow up through the body with no unpleasant side effects.

This powerful energy is in the air that you breath, in the water that you drink, and in all things of nature. In terms of energy field frequencies, it has an extremely high rate of vibration. It can be drawn in through the crown chakra and down into the other major chakras, eventually awakening the *prana* residing near the base chakra. This awakening process is gentle and soothing, allowing the kundalini to flow up the spinal column by way of the sympathetic nervous system, through both the major energy centers and endocrine glands, and then out the crown chakra.

## Crown Chakra Opening Technique

If you wish to do the M-A-Y toning exercise once or twice before you begin, the result may be more effective when performing the following technique.

Get yourself into a comfortable sitting position with your feet placed on the floor or earth beneath you. Do not be concerned with keeping your spine straight or rigid; this is not required. Just make sure that you are in a comfortable chair or even a recliner. If using a reclining position, make sure that your feet dangle or hang down loosely.

Take two or three deep diaphragmatic breaths in and out, in a slow, even manner. Focus on your chest rising and falling as the breath goes in and out.

Now, return to normal breathing and shift your focus from your chest up to the top of the head, where the crown energy center is located.

Keep focusing all your attention here in an area that is about one inch in diameter, about the size of a quarter. Do not worry about focusing in the wrong area; approximation is fine.

As you continue focusing here, start to feel a pressure, a sensation, or even someone's fingers touching your scalp in this region. Then let this sensation or pressure slowly start to expand outwards from one inch in diameter until it completely encompasses all of the top of the head. Feel this sensation, pressure, or in some cases a tingling energy all over the top of the head. For some of you, visualizing a white light or energy all over the top of the head may be as effective as feeling the sensation.

Now, see or feel this tingling energy continuing to spread all through the hair, the scalp, and down the back of the head, down to both ears. In essence, let this sensation, pressure, or tingling energy completely cover all of the head including the forehead or third eye chakra. Let the energy dance all over the head. Feel or see the white light or energy moving all over the head and even feel or see it going inside your head.

Experience the sensation, pressure, or tingling energy all over the head right down to the ears and down the back of the head at the base of the skull.

Focus on this energy or sensation for a few more moments and continue feeling or seeing the white light or energy inside the brain as well.

Finally, take a deep breath in, hold it for a few seconds, and then release it slowly. Let the energy or sensation start to contract until it returns to the size of a quarter, about one inch in diameter on the top of the head. If you need to, see, feel or imagine the white light or energy closing up like the petals of a flower when the sun sets. When you have finished "closing" the crown chakra, you should feel a slight sensation or pressure at the top of the head. This indicates that you have learned to open and close your crown energy center through proper focusing techniques. The slight sensation on the top of the head means that the crown chakra is slightly opened and properly balanced.

> He said to them, "There is light within a person of light, and it shines on the whole world. If it does not shine, it is dark."
> —The sayings of Jesus

## Heart Chakra—Warmth Opening Flower Technique

In chapter 6, you were presented with the Warmth Opening Flower Technique to open and close the heart chakra. Repeat this important technique using the green flower visualization once more. Make sure that you warm up your hands and place the right one over the chest and then do your proper breathing as originally instructed. Feel free to review the heart chakra section in chapter 6.

Once you have completed the Warmth Opening Flower Technique, relax for a few moments, and return to normal breathing before you begin the next special technique.

## Crown to Heart Energy Flow Technique

When you are ready to continue, take a deep breath in and hold it for the count of five, then exhale all your breath gradually out your nostrils. Go back to normal breathing and repeat the Crown Chakra Opening Technique.

This time, as you feel or see the energy or white light fully expanding, let it continue down from the crown center and brain into the third eye center. Focus all your attention on the forehead, feeling or seeing the energy or sensation spreading across the forehead. Keep concentrating on this area, letting the pressure or sensation completely expand until it covers the forehead above the eyebrows. You should feel or see this white light or sensation stretching from temple to temple.

There should now be a more pronounced pressure in the middle of the forehead radiating from the surface of the skin to a depth of about one inch inside the head. This is a sign that the pineal gland has been activated and thus the third eye chakra has opened up.

Concentrate on the third eye for just a few more seconds and then feel or see this sensation, energy, or white light moving slowly down from the forehead into the face. Allow this sensation to continue moving down the face, past the lips, past the chin, and into the throat chakra.

At the throat energy center, start to concentrate all of your attention until you feel, sense, or see a warmth, light, or energy here. Experience the warmth or sensation in this major chakra for a few moments. Let this energy here expand across the throat and through the neck until you can feel or see a light or warm sensation in the middle of the neck.

Enjoy the warmth and light in the throat chakra for three or four more seconds.

Now, start to move this energy, pressure, or sensation down into the upper part of the chest in the heart chakra area.

Let your attention focus completely on the heart energy center. If you desire, place your warm right hand gently onto the chest as previously instructed. This is optional.

It is at this point that you should perform the Warmth Opening Flower Technique again, or you may wish to substitute this particular technique with either the Baby or Loved One Technique. Use whatever exercise that provides the best result for you.

Once you have succeeded in opening the heart center fully, you are now ready to move this warmth, sensation, or light upward. Instead of closing the heart chakra this time, remember to leave it opened to its full capacity. This ensures that all the love and healing energy of the heart chakra will be available for you to direct.

Feel the wonderful warmth or energy in this center for a few seconds. Then start to move this energy back up through the upper chest into the throat center, experiencing the sensation here. Allow this soothing energy or light to continue moving up the throat, into the face. Focus on the sensation as the energy moves through the face and up into the third eye chakra. When it reaches this point, feel or see the white light or energy spreading across the forehead, once again. There is a good possibility that you will feel a pressure in the center of the forehead once more as the pineal gland is activated and the third eye chakra opens fully.

Allow the sensation, pressure, or energy that you feel in the forehead to move up into the crown chakra at the top of the head. Enjoy the wonderful energy or tingling sensation here as it completely encompasses all of the head, including the brain and forehead.

Keep all your attention in this area for just a few seconds and then repeat the process of directing or moving the light or energy back down through the face, the throat chakra, and into the heart center.

When the sensation or energy reaches the heart chakra again, let it spread all across the chest the same as the last time.

When you are ready, direct the energy back up the chest and ultimately to the crown energy center.

Now continue to move this wonderful energy or white light from the crown down to the heart center, and then from this center back up to the crown chakra. Allow the energy to move down and up through these areas for about five minutes or until you feel it is time to stop. At this point, start to focus on the energy, slowing down as it moves up and down the body from the top of the head to the chest. Feel or see this energy or light moving slower and slower until it stops in either the heart chakra or crown chakra; it is your choice whether to use the heart or crown center as the finishing point of this exercise. All you have to do is focus all your attention on either of these major chakras as the energy's momentum slows. Complete this technique by continuing to focus on the heart or crown for a few seconds until you experience either a warm sensation in the heart chakra or a slight pressure or tingling sensation on the top of the head. Then, take a deep breath in, hold it for the count of three and release it slowly and evenly out your nose. Return to normal awareness.

For some of you with difficulty in feeling and moving the chakra energy, focusing on each major chakra one at a time until you feel a warmth, pressure, or sensation there is the best method to try. Once you feel something in the crown chakra, for example, shift your focus to the third eye chakra and repeat the process. Continue, chakra by chakra.

As you feel or sense an energy or warmth in each major chakra from the crown to the heart, you can then start to focus on the warmth in these centers starting to flow in a fluid motion from point to point or energy center to energy center. Eventually, you will be able to speed it up until this healing chakra energy moves up and down through all these centers like warm water flowing through a stream.

## Heart to Base Energy Flow Techniques

You are now ready to try the second phase of the energy flow techniques. All the exercises in chapter 6 and the Crown to Heart Energy Flow Technique that you just completed help to ensure that you will be successful in directing the chakra energy through your body.

Begin the Heart to Base Energy Flow Technique by doing the Warmth Opening Flower Technique on the heart chakra once more.

As you open the beautiful green flower with its petals to their full extension, let it remain open. This ensures that the heart energy center is wide open and the healing energy is ready to move downwards into the solar plexus chakra.

If you wish, you can place your right hand gently over the solar energy center. If the warmth of your palm chakra makes it easier to focus on the solar center, then utilize this. For many of you, it will be easy and natural for you to start moving the warm healing energy or white light from the open heart center down into the solar area.

Concentrate your attention here, feeling or seeing the warmth or energy spreading across the solar plexus chakra. The use of the Warmth Opening Flower Technique may assist you to open this major energy center effectively.

Once you have succeeded in opening up the solar center, start to direct it down past the belly button into the sacral plexus chakra. As before (if you wish to), move your right hand down onto the sacral center, about two to three inches below the navel. Experience the warmth, the energy, or white light here. Feel or see this chakra energy here. Feel or see this chakra energy spreading across the sacral area until it stretches from hip to hip. Use the Warmth Opening Flower Technique here if needed or desired. Remember to visualize an orange flower this time.

Once the warmth, the energy, or the flower expands fully across this major chakra, then let the sensation move down into the base chakra. Feel the warmth or see the white light here. Allow it to expand across into both upper thighs. Then start to move the warm energy or light back up through the sacral chakra. Feel the energy here for a few seconds and then slowly direct it up into the solar energy center, feeling or seeing the warmth or light as it flows through the solar chakra and back up to the heart chakra.

Let the warmth or the energy expand across the chest again. Feel love and warmth in the heart center for a few seconds and then start the process all over. Direct the energy or white light back down through the solar, the sacral, and then into the base.

As it arrives at the base, let it expand from hip to hip once more and then direct it back up through the sacral, past the navel, through the solar, and into the heart chakra.

Repeat the process, moving the warmth or light from the heart back down into the base and from the base back up through to the heart. Keep the chakra energy moving down and up through the body and these chakras for several minutes in a smooth, fluid motion.

When ready, start to slow the chakra energy flow down and finally stop it in the heart center. Focus your attention here for four or five seconds. Now, take in a deep breath, hold it for a moment, and finally release it slowly and evenly out your nose. Return to normal breathing and normal awareness.

As stated in the section dealing with the Crown to Heart Energy Flow Technique, if you have some difficulty feeling and moving the chakra energy properly, focus on one chakra at a time until you feel the warmth or sensation there. Then move your focus to the next chakra and continue concentrating until you receive the same results. Do the focusing technique chakra by chakra—heart, solar, sacral, and base—and then start to speed the energy up until the chakra energy flows in a smooth, fluid manner up and down all these major chakras.

The more you practice this, the easier it will be to move and direct energy flow through your body. You will become like the natural "feelers," moving the chakra energy through your body and chakras in an easy and beneficial manner.

When you become proficient at directing chakra energy through your body and major chakras you will trigger the kundalini energy stored at the base area. This will arouse the energy and it will start to flow up through the sympathetic nervous system, the body, the endocrine glandular system, the major chakras, and ultimately out the top of the head. The kundalini and chakra energy will start to flow as one unified energy.

Feeling or seeing white light, warmth, or energy in the special energy flow techniques given to you will actually start the chakra energy and kundalini to awaken and flow properly.

You have now learned the power of focusing on parts of your body and directing real healing energy through it.

## Crown to Base Energy Flow Technique

This technique is the final one, the most important technique to use. It will become clear that it is a combination of the two previous techniques just given to you.

When you begin the Crown to Base Energy Flow Technique, you can use either the crown or heart center as a starting point. The reason for giving you a choice is quite simple.

Some of you may find it easier to begin this exercise by focusing on the crown chakra, letting this center activate and open up. On the other hand, many of you may find it easier to focus on the heart chakra, using the special exercises given to you for this center and thereby opening the heart chakra up.

In either case, you will continue by directing the energy, warmth, or light down through the major chakras and then back up again.

Essentially, you will be repeating the exercises given to you in the Crown to Heart Energy Flow and the Heart to Base Energy Flow Techniques.

As you start this meditation technique at either the crown or heart center, direct the warmth, sensation, or light all the way down to the base chakra. Once the energy reaches here, let it move back up through all the major chakras and into the crown center. Feel the tingling sensation all over your head or visualize a white light or energy covering the crown area.

Now move the chakra energy down through all the chakras again until you arrive at the root or base center. Feel the energy or warmth expanding across the upper thighs and hips. Then send the energy up through the major energy centers into the top of the head once more.

Repeat the process, directing the chakra energy or light down and up through the body and energy centers.

Feel free to place your right hand gently on top of the heart chakra, then the solar and finally the sacral chakra. While you do this, use the warmth of your palm chakra as a focal point while you move the energy from center to center.

You can also allow the heart, solar, sacral, and base chakras to open up fully by doing the Warmth Opening Flower Technique on each of these centers if desired.

Use any or all of these methods for the best results possible as you continue to direct the light, warmth, and energy up and down the body through all the chakras.

Once the chakra energy has developed into a smooth, fluid flow, direct it into the base again, allowing the warmth or sensation to spread across the upper thighs as before. This time move the energy down the legs, past the knees, and down into both feet.

Sense the energy here on the bottom of each foot where the feet chakras are located. The bottom of each foot has an energy center similar to the palm chakras of the hands. Feel or see the energy of the earth, Mother Earth, coming up through these chakras into the legs, the thighs, and finally into the base chakra. As the power of the earth arrives into this chakra, experience the energy, the warmth, and power pulsing here. Kundalini has now been fully aroused! Then move this kundalini energy along with the chakra energy up through the centers and into the crown chakra at the top of the head.

As before, feel or see the white light or energy all over the head and then direct it back down through to the base, finally into the feet. Let the earth energy move up once more, feeling or seeing the energy flowing through all of your body, your chakras, and into the crown.

Allow all of these combined energies, earth, Universal, kundalini, and chakra energies to flow down and up through the body from the top of the head to the bottom of the feet.

Enjoy the sensation, warmth, and peace as this wonderful energy continues to flow like a warm, gentle stream up and down through the body, the chakras, and even your spinal column.

Some of you will be fortunate enough to experience rushes of energy up and down the spine as the chakra energy, as well as the other energies move through the chakra system and body.

Do this energy flow work for about five minutes at the very most, then begin to slow the energy down. Let the energy continue to slow down and then have it stop in either your heart or crown center. Focus all your attention on either chakra for several seconds. Experience a warmth in the upper chest or a tingling sensation on top of the head. Then take a deep breath, hold it for three seconds, and  release the breath. Return to normal consciousness.

In most cases, all of the major energy centers will automatically close down a bit, but will remain slightly open and balanced. This allows the healing essence of the body to remain in these centers for health and harmony.

For those individuals who are natural "feelers," doing the Crown to Base Energy Flow Technique will be effortless, natural, and pleasurable. You may find that you can bypass the Crown to Heart Energy Flow and the Heart to Base Energy Flow Techniques and go directly to this important meditation technique.

For individuals who experience some difficulty performing the energy work at first, following the steps as outlined in this chapter and the previous one will assist you in opening up your chakras and starting the energy flow. The more you practice these techniques, the easier and more natural the results.

The Crown to Base Energy Flow Technique should be done on a weekly if not daily basis. This chakra energy work should become part of your regimen in life.

Incidentally, every time you do the Crown to Base Energy Flow Technique, your life will become more peaceful and harmonious. Events, circumstances, and life's situations seem to flow easier for about three days after practicing this technique. This energy helps to change you, how you feel, and also how people around you feel about you and react to you. You learn to "gentle" your own aura, chakras, and thereby release a more peaceful and serene energy from your being. People will start to notice the change, the positive difference in you as you continue to do chakra energy flow work. You will start to develop a beautiful, bright, and clean aura that emanates a powerful yet gentle energy. This loving energy around you will start to affect others in a subtle but profound way, helping them to advance onto a spiritual path themselves.

## The Sympathetic Nervous Division

The human body consists of two nervous systems, known as the central or spinal nervous system, and the autonomic nervous system.

The latter nervous system is of primary importance in regards to healing and chakra energy. The autonomic nervous system contains two divisions, the sympathetic and the parasympathetic. The sympathetic nervous division is directly connected with the chakras, the human aura, and the Universal and Mother Earth energies.

As mentioned earlier, the sympathetic division is in "sympathy" or harmony with these higher vibrations and God the Creator.

The two sympathetic nerve trunks, which contain both the sympathetic and parasympathetic nervous divisions, exist on both sides of the spinal column, which of course contains the central nervous system.

Both nervous systems are connected to each other by groups of nerves called "ganglia." This remarkable arrangement ensures that vital nerve energy is able to flow between both nervous systems and, consequently, throughout the whole body.

Additionally, the sympathetic nervous division is linked to the human chakra system via nerve bundles or ganglia. These nerves are able to harmonize or resonate with the very high vibratory rates of the seven major chakras. The vibrational energies of these chakras are able to "step-down" or lower their vibratory rates as their energy flows into these nerves. From this point, the ganglia direct the "lowered" chakra vibrations into the central nervous system, the endocrine glandular system, and to essentially all of the physical body including the cells.

Likewise, lower vibration energies of the physical level such as illness, pain, or disease can flow out from the glands, organs, cells, muscles, and central nervous system of the body into the sympathetic nervous division, and ultimately into the major chakra or chakra closely associated with the afflicted physical area. This essence or negative energy will also spread from the chakra or chakras into the human aura. This is why aura readers and medical intuitives are able to discern the negative colors in a person's aura or chakras.

In essence, the sympathetic nervous division functions like a two way street allowing various energies to flow either way.

By understanding the sympathetic nervous division and the principle just mentioned you would be able to recognize the value of performing chakra energy flow techniques.

The kundalini, chakra, universal and earth energies flow up and down through the seven major chakras, the sympathetic nervous division, the endocrine glandular system and finally into all of the human body. This is a powerful, healing tool that can also be used for spiritual enlightenment.

> A sensible man would remember that the eyes may be confused in two ways, and for two reasons—by a change from light to darkness, or from darkness to light. He will consider that the same will happen with the soul . . .
> —Plato (Greek philosopher, fifth and fourth centuries B.C.E.)

# Chapter 8

# *Channeling: Working With Your Angels and Spirit Guides*

For He will give His angels charge concerning
you, to guard you in all your ways.
—Psalms 91:11

Angels and spirit guides have been part of our world for thousands of years. These beings of light have influenced many cultures, both past and present. They have helped to bring a part of heaven to earth.

In this chapter, you will be learning techniques to work with your angels and spirit guides. Nowadays, the general term applied to this phenomena is "channeling." In the past, it was sometimes referred to as spiritual mediumship, or communication with the dead. These two references are not entirely accurate terms. In truth, there is much more to channeling than mere communication with spirit guides or people who have left this physical realm. Being ignorant of the truth, our society refers to these people as being dead.

If you wish to understand the truth, you must first understand that in reality there is no death. Yes, the physical body—the form—may age and die, but the soul that resides within is immortal and everlasting. Our friends and loved ones never really die. They simply move on to a higher dimension of existence commonly referred to as heaven or the heavenly fields. This concept will be discussed later.

## The Difference Between Angels and Spirit Guides

Many people confuse the words angels and spirit guides when talking or thinking about these light beings. Countless numbers of people believe that they are one and the same: an angel is a spirit guide and a spirit guide is an angel.

Even though these beings work together with each other and in some cases perform similar tasks or missions, they are not the same. Angels and spirit guides do not belong in the same phylum or order.

Some people also believe that a special person possessing saintly qualities may in fact be an angel on earth or will become one when he or she passes over to the other side into heaven. The fact is an angel is an angel and has been and always will be one.

These celestial beings are the unique creation of God the Creator. They have a divine connection with the Creator and perform numerous tasks on behalf of the heavenly realms. Angels can heal, comfort, protect, and guide you throughout your life.

These spiritual beings are also heavenly messengers that herald news or warnings to people. The word angel comes from the Greek word *aggelos* or *angelos*, which means "messenger."

There are many references to these celestial beings in both the New and Old Testament, over 300 in all. In the early chapters of Matthew and Luke, for instance, the archangel Gabriel visits Zechariah, the future father of John the Baptist, as well as the Virgin Mary, the future mother of Jesus. This special messenger from heaven announces the upcoming births of John the Baptist and Jesus, respectively. Warnings are also attributed to angels in the Bible.

The heavenly fields above contain different levels or dimensions. Everything and everyone exists here at an extremely high rate of vibration. There is also a hierarchy in heaven that begins with God, the God force—known as the Creator or Supreme Being.

It is here at the core or center that the Creator, consisting of both male and female principles, radiates divine energy outwards into the heavenly realms and ultimately down into the universe, the stars, the planets, and the earth. This divine essence possessing intelligence, power, and healing energy permeates both the higher spiritual vibrations of heaven and the lower physical vibrations of Earth.

It is the angels of God that move and work in both realms. They are as numerous as the stars, are unique, and have different missions or purposes.

Some of these special beings work as guardian angels, protecting individuals during their lifetimes. In fact, many small children can see their own guardian angels and accept these celestial spirits with open and innocent hearts (see chapter 2). Even organized Christianity, with all its faults, now embraces this concept.

The hierarchy of heaven consists of an established order of angels, starting with the archangels who possess wondrous powers and are responsible for all the other angels. The archangels are very close to the presence of the Creator and perform very special missions, taking on the attributes of important divine messengers, miracle workers, great healers, protectors, spiritual teachers, and warriors against the darkness of evil.

# Angels

Four of the best known of these powerful, loving beings are Raphael, Gabriel, Uriel, and Michael. Gifted clairvoyants and others can see and sense these beings of light. Some people blessed with clairaudient abilities can hear angels and spirit guides talking to them.

Hopefully, you will gain these abilities yourself, using the technique that will be taught to you in this chapter. Starting with the information given here, you can develop the special clairvoyant and clairaudient abilities needed in order to see and communicate with your angels and spirit guides.

Your angels will also work with you in strange yet wondrous ways. Gifted healers or persons who have and desire to use this potential will be able to start working with healing angels. As your crown, third eye, heart, and palm chakras activate and open up, you will receive the healing energy from the heavenly planes as well as the presence and healing power of a healing angel or angels. These celestial beings possess healing gifts and can "vibrate down" from the higher realms or lower their frequencies, descending into this physical realm where they will join their energies with your auric fields.

As the natural healers among you develop your skills you will raise the vibrations of both the body and the human aura. The aura will expand and if the crown chakra has been activated properly, a healing angel will enter into your energy field and link with both the crown and third eye centers. This celestial spirit will then work through you, bringing healing and Universal Energy down through the crown, into your heart chakra (which should now be opened with love). From here, the healing energy from this angel, along with the other energy, will flow down your arms, into the hands, and out the palms and fingers. Essentially, you will have increased the amount of healing energy flowing through you and out of your body into your patient or client. This ensures that the person receiving the treatment will be able to use more external healing essence in order to trigger the release of his or her own internal healing energies. Your client or patient will be aware of this increase of energy flowing from you.

The above scenario is one of the reasons why the previous exercises were presented to you. When your chakras are opened properly, more of your abilities manifest more easily. Healing with angels as just described is actually a form of channeling. These special beings of light can, in some cases, enter the room where a healing session or treatment is being conducted and place their angelic hands on a client or patient. The person experiencing the healing session will feel additional pairs of hands on his or her body. This form of angelic healing will become the norm as more people with natural healing abilities awaken and raise the vibrations of their auras, chakras, and physical bodies.

Some of these celestial beings visit the bedsides of the sick and perform special work while these people sleep; miraculous healings can be the results. Even people who have survived near death experiences (NDEs) report the presence of angels or beings of light during these profound events.

There are also angels assigned to people who are about to pass over to the other side. As a person's body is dying, the individual will start to see or sense the presence of angels, spirit guides, and loved ones. Perhaps his or her guardian angel will appear in the room along with a departed grand-mother or grandfather. This visitation will normally occur a day or two before the death of the human body. It is a way to prepare the human soul of that person for the transition from the earthly realm into the higher vibrations of heaven. In many cases, the individual will become peaceful and be comforted at this time. He or she is also more psychically attuned with the higher dimensions and may very well exist in a place between heaven and earth. In any event, the soul of the person is never alone at the point of physical death. An angel of death will then escort the human soul—the true being within—out of the physical form, and both the angel and the newly departed soul will raise their vibrations and ascend into the heavenly fields.

In the past, certain Tibetan Buddhists monks were trained to assist the departing soul over to the "other side." There are also some very special clairvoyants and sensitives that are now able to perform this particular function. In the near future, there will be individuals working at this specialized task in a full-time, professional capacity.

Most major religions believe in the existence of angels. Angels are mentioned in the Jewish tradition and the reli-gion of Islam accepts the reality of these divine beings. In fact, the prophet Muhammad claimed to have had a vision of the archangel Gabriel who promised to help him in his teaching.

These angelic beings can also be seen in art. During the Renaissance, many famous artists created masterpieces that contained both religious figures and angels. In 1618, Leonardo Da Vinci painted *The Annunciation* ("Detail of the Angel"), a beautiful work of art portraying an angel with wings and a halo (i.e., an aura). This is only one of the numerous paintings of angels that were completed during the birth of modern Western civilization.

In more recent times, there has been an increased interest in these beings of light. There is a good reason for this. As more people awaken, they will become more aware of spiritual matters while they are less concerned with mundane affairs of the physical world. Working with angels and spirit guides too will be a common occurrence.

Angels are the bearers of love, light, comfort, and reassurance for many. For children, they are guardians and companions. Without these beings of love and light our world would be a sad place of mere existence; no one would truly "live."

> Silently one by one, in the infinite meadow of Heaven, Blossomed the lovely stars, the forget-me-nots of the angels.
> —Henry W. Longfellow (poet, 1807–82)

## Spirit Guides

Spirit guides work in conjunction with the angels. Both share similarities with each other when assisting humans on the earthly plane. Spirit guides perform duties such as guiding, teaching, and comforting people.

There is a very close relationship between the human family and spirit guides. Unlike angels, guides have existed in human form in the past. They have lived, felt, and experienced the emotions associated with living in the physical on Earth. These beings no longer possess a physical body and now function in their true essence as souls, possessing higher rates of vibrations than people do.

There are many people who, during a good portion of their earthly sojourn, will be guided, comforted, and assisted by departed loved ones such as grandfathers, grandmothers, and other late relatives and friends. In fact, some North American Indians refer to this experience as "walking with the grandfathers"; aboriginal people in Australia hold similar beliefs.

Generally speaking, when human beings die or, rather, have their souls pass over into heaven, they experience a life review and examine all aspects of that recent lifetime. A time of rest and recovery may be in order for many newly departed souls.

Spirit guides, like human beings, come from "all walks of life." They have their unique personalities and idiosyncrasies, just as with human beings. They are merely souls without physical bodies who have agreed or wished to work with people. This service to humankind is provided so that spirit guides can grow and evolve towards their own true enlightenment.

These guides, therefore, are not infallible. They too have their faults just like you. Spirit guides, especially the ones in training, come here to earth to learn and experience situations. All people have spirit guides around them as well as angels. And, like angels, there are many different types of these spiritual beings or guides.

Some of you will have a few guides helping you at any one time. Others of you will have numerous guides around you to assist in your tasks and life experiences. The number of spirit guides working with you is directly proportional to what you are doing at a particular time in your life, where you are on your spiritual path and at what rate of vibration or frequency your body, aura, and chakras are.

Certain spirit guides possess skills such as are found in physician healers, business managers, accountants, orators, teachers, and so forth. They will work specifically with individuals who need assistance in these distinct areas of expertise.

All souls in heaven continue the learning process and work on their spiritual growth. There is more of an understanding of the earthly and heavenly realms by these souls who are not encumbered by physical bodies. All are aware of many of their previous human incarnations and perform certain duties while inhabiting the heavenly fields. Some may even be aware of former lifetimes on other planets or in the physical realm.

Wise, loving teachers are assigned to them in order to help them develop into more enlightened souls; many angels assist in these teachings as well. While in heaven, human souls visit different places and different vibrational levels where universal knowledge and higher healing energies exist.

As people on the physical plane visit libraries that house books and information for the purpose of learning, human souls in heaven go to the Akashic Records, also known as the Universal Storehouse of Knowledge to access information that is pertinent for them and their soul growth.

When ready, certain souls in heaven make preparations to return or reincarnate into a physical body. There are many beings in heaven associated with this procedure. Angels, special teachers, or guides, as well as the Council of Elders all work together to prepare the human soul to return to earth.

The soul makes an arrangement or agrees to a "spiritual contract" to return to the physical realm, where he or she hovers in and out of a prospective mother's aura and womb. This is why pregnant women often seem to have a glow about them: they have both their auric field as well as the aura of the unborn soul surrounding the body.

Finally, at or just prior to birth, the human soul—after extensive preparation—will settle fully into the body of the child. Although the soul will hover in and out of the unborn child's body during the pregnancy, the soul will join with the body and the two will become one. Thus a human soul now exists within a physical body. The reincarnation process has been repeated.

There are some human souls in the heavenly fields who decide to become spirit guides rather than return physically to earth; in some cases, these souls will be asked to work in this capacity. All of this takes training and preparation.

## The Elohim or Council of Elders

A body of spirits known as the Elohim or Council of Elders exists on a higher vibration or level in the heavenly fields than the spirit guides. There are a total of twelve wise and ancient beings, twelve souls that sit on this important council at any given time. Many equally wise souls in light bodies work with the Elohim as an extension of this council.

Jesus had his council or inner circle of twelve along with many other disciples on earth, all cooperating together as a special organization nearly 2,000 years ago. On the physical level, this organization was based on the structure of the Council of Elders as they are arranged in the higher realms. This is why the number twelve was important for Jesus during his lifetime as a master teacher.

The Elohim function as coordinators and regulators of human souls, spirit guides, and some angels (in unique cases). They are responsible for harmony and balance in both heaven and earth. This relates directly to the birth and death process associated with reincarnation, with the selection, training, and guidance of spirit guides, and with the evolution and spiritual growth of human souls.

These wise souls on the Council are fully knowledgeable on the matters of the possible future of earth and humankind. Many of them are old teachers, old souls, and old masters who lived on the earth many eons ago. The archangels work closely with them in many instances.

## Walking on the Spiritual Path

The changes that take place when entering on a spiritual path or search have already been discussed in brief. When you begin to practice chakra energy work, meditation, and deep soul searching, your aura will become stronger, cleaner, and brighter. Your chakras, especially your crown, third eye, and heart centers, will activate and open up. Your physical body will start to change, to become lighter. On a psychological level, your conscious and subconscious thought patterns will change positively.

As these things begin to happen, your aura, chakras, body, and whole being will begin vibrating at a higher rate. In essence, you will raise your frequency or vibratory rate, making it easier for your spirit guides and angels to help you and work with you on the physical earth. As your vibratory rates increase, spirit guides possessing higher energy will start to work with you and channel their power, gifts, and energies through you.

You will also begin to experience the tremendous power, love, and healing energy of angels as your vibratory rate or frequency steps up. The raising of your consciousness and the raising of your vibrations are required if you wish to receive and handle the potent energy of angels.

The world we live in is changing its vibrations as well. It is increasing its frequency and becoming closer in vibratory rate to some of the heavenly fields or dimensions. This means, essentially, that the expression "heaven on earth" is becoming more than mere words.

It is now time to cover specific channeling techniques that you can use to assist in learning the channeling technique and thus work with your angels and spirit guides.

## Raising the Vibrations of Your Environment Technique

Before doing any type of channeling you need to ensure that the room, home, or area where you are practicing has a peaceful, high level of energy. The vibrations of the place should be raised sufficiently. This creates a peaceful, harmonious, and safe environment for your channeling and meditation purposes.

Many people are careless in this regard. They simply channel or become spirit mediums without taking any proper preparatory steps. This, in some cases, will result in connection with lower entities or spirits of an undesirable nature; remember, not all beings of a nonphysical source come from the Light (God). Therefore, it is important to raise the vibratory rate or energy within your environment in order to protect yourself and guarantee that angels and more enlightened spirit guides will manifest here.

The first step to raise the vibrations of your environment involves simple yet effective use of certain articles. White or light-colored candles; incense such as sandalwood or frankincense; and soft, gentle music are all crucial. The combination of all or any of these items helps to raise the vibrations within a room, an enclosed space or designated area. One traditional Native American tradition, "smudging," uses sage and sweetgrass in place of incense; this practice is recommended if you do not care for incense.

After you have lit the candles, incense, and put on some peaceful, soothing music, you are ready for the next step. Make sure that the music is heard only in the background: it should not be too loud and can range from classical to new age, depending on your taste and what you find soothing.

The power of the voice has been discussed in earlier chapters. If used in the right way, your voice can literally change or raise the vibrations of energy in a room. The ancient Egyptians and Tibetan Buddhists were fully aware of this potential power within.

The organized Christian Church, with its rituals using candles, incense, and sounds, creates the right vibrations within an enclosed space, a church building; unfortunately, the Church officials are often unaware of the true reason for their ritualistic practices. Upon entering a church from the street, most individuals can readily feel the high energy in a church, especially if the structure is a lofty cathedral. This is the proper energy or high vibratory rate that is needed for proper effective channeling.

God the Creator is a combination of two principles consisting of male and female essences. These essences are also referred to as positive (male) and negative (female). This is the same concept found in the scientific laws of magnetism and electricity: both parts are needed to create a manifestation. Chinese philosophy calls these qualities ying (male) and yang (female), and is concerned with the balance of life and harmony through this arrangement.

Neophytes or students entering into the Egyptian Mystery Schools and healing temples were taught this principle. They were also taught a special vowel chant or intonation to create this balance and harmony and raise the energy within a room or enclosed space.

This vowel chant is MAH-RAH. MAH is the female, negative, or mother principle, and RAH is the male, positive, or father principle. The MAH-RAH chant should be done in a mid-C musical note. As stated before, if you are not musically inclined do not worry; an approximation is fine when chanting this sound. Simply try to keep your voice at a midrange, not too high and not too low.

Begin by placing yourself in the center of your chosen room or enclosed area, or as close to the center as possible.

Get relaxed and then take in a deep breath through your nose. Hold the breath in for about five seconds, then release it slowly and evenly out the nostrils or mouth.

Once again take in a deep breath and hold it for a few seconds. This time as you release the breath slowly through the mouth chant M-m-a-a-h-h-h–R-r-a-a-h-h-h, letting it be released as two long musical notes. Allow the chant to continue until all your air has been expelled. Try to make sure that both the tones of MAH and RAH are chanted or sung for about the same intervals. Wait a few seconds and then take in another deep breath, and hold it for a few seconds again.

This time, tone or chant R-r-a-a-h-h-h–M-m-a-a-h-h-h instead of MAH-RAH. In other words, simply alternate MAH-RAH with RAH-MAH, letting the RAH or father principle sound begin the chant.

Continue chanting this ancient sound for a total of five to ten times in your room. Each time you go through the process of toning MAH-RAH, alternate it from MAH-RAH to RAH-MAH, and then MAH-RAH until you have completed the required five to ten repetitions of this chant.

After the final chant, find a comfortable place to sit and then just relax. In about one to two minutes, the vibratory rate within the room will rise dramatically. Your may notice that the flames of the lit candles will start to increase in height; you might even feel a slight tingle on the back of your neck or a warm feeling in your heart or solar plexus centers. A peaceful feeling should start to settle over you. These are all indications of the subtle yet positive energy change in the room.

You have now succeeded in the first step to proper and safe channeling: raising the vibrations of your environment.

Incidentally, the Raising the Vibrations of Your Environment Technique can be used in your home, office, or business environment. This technique can be performed in each room of your house, thus raising the energy of your whole home to a high, peaceful, and harmonious level.

The Mah-Rah chant can also be used in your office, store, or any work environment. It has a subtle effect on people and the environment they inhabit. As the energy rises, the room, office, or area will develop a peaceful, harmonious, and inviting presence. Friends, coworkers, customers, or patients will be affected by this change in the atmosphere. They will become more relaxed and more at peace in the vicinity of this higher energy. For business purposes, this wonderful technique will increase business, drawing people into the office, store, or other work area.

At first, the Mah-Rah chant should be done about five to ten times in these places. After that, the toning can be done three or four times in succession, about once a week. This exercise, when practiced on a regular basis, will slowly continue to build up high energy in the area. Eventually, the place will maintain a constant, high vibratory rate, making people feel very peaceful and calm. Coworkers will get along better with one another; individuals will seem more cooperative.

If you feel the need to perform this technique more often, do so; it cannot be overdone. A home or any other place that has chaotic energy will take longer to change into better vibrations. In these cases, more chanting of the MAH-RAH may be necessary.

This special exercise, if done by two or more people in a specific room or area where violence, turmoil, sadness, and grief have come to reside, will heal, change, and raise these lower vibrations to a gentler, loving, higher vibration of energy.

## Raising Your Vibrations Techniques

The next important step before channeling is to raise your own vibrations. There are several methods of accomplishing this.

In chapter 3, you were taught the Crown Chakra Exercise that involved the chanting of MAY. This chant can be done once or twice in order to open up the crown chakra, thus making it easier to channel and receive the vibrational energies associated with your spirit guides and angels.

When this center opens up, the third eye chakra will do likewise. These "opened" chakras will result in higher vibrations in both the crown and third eye.

After this, you can also perform any of the techniques that pertain to the heart chakra such as the Heart Chakra Opening Technique or the Baby Technique.

By focusing on the heart chakra, you will open it up and raise the vibrations here, and throughout your whole body. The warm, healing energy of the heart chakra associated with love will be very effective in raising the vibrations of your whole being. This is important for working with spirit guides who possess high, loving energy that is directly linked to the Creator and the heavenly fields.

If you wish, you can do some crown to base chakra energy work next. The complete chakra energy flow exercise is not required but it is beneficial in expanding your aura and making it easier to work with your guides and angels. A strong, vibrant, and clean human energy field draws loving beings of light toward you.

The final exercise that you should perform prior to channeling involves the heart chakra once again. In this case, you will simply focus your attention on the heart center, thinking of the word "love." Concentrate on your heart and this word for about ten or fifteen seconds. Next, start to either say out loud or think the phrase: "love fills my heart and my soul." Keep saying or thinking these words for a minute or two, and try to feel the love within your heart chakras and your whole essence.

When you feel that you have done this exercise long enough, stop. Take in a deep breath, hold it for a few seconds, and then release it slowly and evenly out of your mouth or nose. Following this, just relax for a bit.

Once you have completed some or all of these techniques, you will have succeeded in raising your own vibrations to a much higher level. Your body, your cells, your chakras, and your aura are all at a higher frequency, allowing the spirit guides and angels to lower their vibratory rates and connect with you at a midpoint between your normal earthly vibrations and their normal heavenly vibrations.

Upon raising the vibrations of your immediate environment and yourself, you are now ready to start channeling.

# Channeling Techniques

You should always make sure that all negative thoughts are put aside just before channeling; this includes worries, fears, anger, sadness, and unhappy thoughts. You should be relaxed and at relative peace.

# White Light Meditation

Get into the habit of visualizing white light surrounding both you and your environment on a weekly (if not daily) basis.

This is a very simple meditation or visualization exercise. Allow yourself to become relaxed. Shut your eyes for a few moments and picture your surroundings in your mind. Then, let a circle of white light completely envelop the room or place where you are, fully encircling everything. From this point, encircle your body from head to toe in a sheath of white light. Allow yourself to be absorbed by this circle or sheath of white energy that now resides within another circle of white light.

When you practice this meditation, you are learning to literally draw in the high vibrations of the white energy around you and your environment. *This is not your imagination!* This technique helps to protect you by keeping lower entities and negative spirits from entering into your special place of meditation or, for that matter, any other area that has white light protection.

You can even perform this exercise on your vehicle prior to traveling anywhere. Ensure that both you and anyone within the vehicle are covered in white light, too.

The exercises given to you in earlier chapters to awaken your psychic abilities are also responsible for the increased mental capabilities of your brain. As your mental power increases, you start working more effectively with thought vibrations. In essence, your ability to think of something and then create that thought on the physical plane becomes very real and very powerful. That is why you are able to bring in the higher vibrations of white light when you visualize it surrounding you and your environment.

Thoughts are real, so be careful what you think and how you think. Learn to think and say positive things instead. The old adage is very true: "As you think, so you create."

It is advisable at this time to create a special list of positive affirmations. Write them down, read them and then memorize these affirmations. Start to say them under your breath or in your mind on a regular basis. Continue this regimen for about thirty days and then cease the exercise.

These positive affirmations will slowly start to enter your subconscious mind from your conscious thoughts. In about thirty to forty days afterwards, you will notice a subtle yet pleasant change within your thought processes. The constructive thoughts or affirmations will have been absorbed into the subconscious mind creating, healthy thought patterns here and also in the conscious mind.

With the increase of your mental powers (along with these powerful changes), you will be able to create more beneficial events and material items in your physical world.

## Candle And Mirror Technique (Extension)

In chapter 5, you were given the Candle and Mirror Technique, Phase One, in order to learn how to see auras. This technique can also be used as a channeling exercise.

## Phase One

This time when you try the Phase One of this technique, you will remain longer in front of the mirror, staring through your eyes as if you are looking into the distance. As you enter into a deeper state of consciousness or a light trance state, you will notice once more that your face in the mirror is starting to shift and change before your eyes. The nose may start to appear longer or perhaps your eyebrows seem to move higher. This is nothing to be concerned with as this is the desired effect. This is an indication that you are now in a deeper, altered state of consciousness.

You will probably start to notice something unusual occurring at this point: the facial shifts will become more prominent and then another face will appear in the reflection. It will look like an overlay of one face placed lightly over your own facial expressions, much the same as a photographic overlay. The eyes that you see before you will suddenly start to take on a different shape. These eyes will look entirely different than your own. Perhaps, the eyes will look Asian, or more rounded, or they may look like the eyes of an old man or woman.

As you continue watching while in this trance state, your eyes may gravitate towards either the left or right eye in the reflected vision. Just allow this to happen and keep gazing at the reflection.

Now, as the eyes keep changing, you will also notice the whole face doing the same thing. You may see a young boy or girl gazing back at you, or even a gray-bearded man doing the same. These facial shifts will continue with you receiving or seeing anywhere from five or six different facial expressions—persons staring back at you—to countless different faces.

Each of you will have different experiences from the Candle and Mirror Technique, Phase One. The facial shifts will occur by appearing one after another, either slowly or in rapid succession. In rare circumstances, some of you might see the face of an animal looking back at you. This too is fine.

Continue gazing through the image in the mirror for a few more moments. The shifting of some of these facial overlays will slow down and may even stop on one particular facial feature. If this happens, you should observe the face before you for a few seconds, paying attention to details. It will feel like you know this person or face looking back at you, almost as if this feature is part of you. This familiarity will create a sense of contentment within as you keep staring at the vision before you.

Soon, the vision will start to disappear and then, if you are fortunate, everything in the mirror will become dark to the point that you will not be able to see your own face or any other features anymore. The scene before you will be totally black for a second or two. Then, if you are deep enough into a midtrance state, a pair of beautiful eyes will appear before you. Let yourself look right through these beautiful eyes directly in front of you.

This phenomena is called "touching the eyes of your soul." It means that you have altered your brainwave patterns to a much lower cycle, entered into a deep alpha state or "trauma" (i.e., dreaming) state, and have connected with the higher self, the "true you" within. You have succeeded in putting the ego or the false persona aside and allowed yourself to look into your soul. The connection lets you become one with your higher being and puts you in touch with the powerful and loving "real you." Once this occurs, you will be able to repeat the exercise more often and continue to grow spiritually by putting the ego aside and slowly letting the real being within come through to the surface. This is a form of true awakening.

Incidentally, the different facial features that you observed during the Candle and Mirror Technique, Phase One, were either spirit guides or angels looking back at you in the mirror, or possibly one of your past life personalities showing through.

If the facial overlay or feature appears without any feeling of pressure, sensation, or tingling on the top of your head (in the crown chakra), and there is no sensation of being filled with energy from the crown to the heart center, then you are simply experiencing who you were in a previous lifetime; if the face you are seeing seems to remain in your vision for a few moments and there is a sense of familiarity, then you are bringing an important past life to the surface. This is a previous incarnation that has a great impact on your life now either on a conscious or subconscious level.

However, if it is a spirit guide or angel gazing back at you, then you will have felt a pressure, sensation, or even a tingling energy upon the top of the head and then experienced a warm, loving energy starting to move from the crown chakra, through your head, your brain, your face, and down past the throat chakra into the heart center where a warmth or peaceful sensation will be enjoyed. You might even experience an energy flow or rush from the crown all the way down to your base chakra or feet. This is the high vibratory energy of your spirit guides or angels working through your aura and chakras.

If it is an angel working through you, the tremendous energy pouring through from the crown will be almost overwhelming in some situations. On the other hand, if a spirit guide is channeling through you, the energy will be less powerful but just as loving and beneficial.

Once you have experienced this joining of your self with one of your spirit guides or angels, you will be able to meet and channel any of their energies and essences on a regular basis in the future. This first connection is the most important one because the door between your earthly realm and the heavenly fields opens at this time and lets you function on both realms in one manner or another.

The first few times that you practice the Candle and Mirror Technique, Phase One, may result in sore or red eyes after five minutes of mirror gazing. This is a normal occurrence for many; with more practice, the soreness and redness will disappear as you become used to mirror gazing for long intervals of time.

When you have completed all of Phase One of this extension technique, you can either stop by taking in a deep breath, holding it for a few seconds, then releasing the breath, slowly letting yourself return to normal consciousness; or you can move on to Phase Two. The more you try this exercise, the easier it is to channel your guides and angels, as well as to experience both past life memories and personalities.

## Phase Two

In chapter 5 on "Reading and Interpreting the Human Aura," the Candle and Mirror Technique, Phase Two, was covered in detail. Please review this technique if you feel that it is required.

The technique also contained a special crown chakra focusing exercise for you to open and expand this energy center. Make sure that you repeat this exercise as you do the complete Phase Two technique.

Once you have completed all of this technique you can now start the final phase of the Candle and Mirror Technique.

## Phase Three

This is an entirely new technique that has not been discussed before. Continue to look above your head at the expanded crown chakra and expanded auric field for a few seconds.

Now move your gaze up even higher, about another six to twelve inches above. As you position your eyes in this area outside of the aura either directly above your head or just off to the side, you will start to notice a human-shaped silhouette of light blue, white, or light yellow floating in space. This silhouette consisting of one of these beautiful colors in a transparent (i.e., not solid) form is one of your spirit guides, or perhaps even an angel hovering above you just outside of your energy field.

Keep focusing on your guide of light for a few moments, feeling his or her presence and loving energy. Then, either out loud or in your mind, ask for this being of light to descend into your auric field, chakra system, and body.

Watch in quiet anticipation as your spirit guide or even your guardian angel starts to move downwards through the top of your expanded aura and crown center. You will see the shape of a head and shoulders consisting of white light start to join with the light of your crown chakra. This area above and surrounding your head will become even brighter and will expand further outwards as your spirit guide or angel descends into your auric field via the crown center.

You will also feel a tingling sensation, pressure, or strange energy on the top of your head in the crown chakra as this connection takes place (this phenomenon was discussed earlier).

Enjoy this energy as your guide or angel settles within your auric field and some or all of your chakras. You should feel peaceful, relaxed, and balanced as you "start to channel" your guide. Usually, the crown, third eye, throat, and heart centers are affected. When you look at your reflection in the mirror, it will appear different: there will be a superimposed image of this being of light over top of your own facial features.

Gaze at this loving presence in the mirror and feel the loving essence of this being of light. You might start to hear words, either in your own voice or in someone else's, talking inside your head. If it is the voice of someone else it will be distinctively male or female, depending on the personality working through you. If the voice sounds like your own, it will be slightly different than your normal voice. In any case, pay attention to what you are hearing.

Sometimes only a few words will be heard. In some cases a few sentences or paragraphs will be spoken in your mind.

In many situations, however, a great deal of information will be heard as your clairaudient abilities increase. Get into the habit of recording the channeled information into a journal on a regular basis. This allows you the opportunity to review these words from "on high."

Some of these channeled words will be of a personal nature, while in other cases they will be related to situations of a prophetic nature. This information may contain wisdom and knowledge that is needed by yourself and others. Words of guidance and encouragement will also come forth.

Many individuals may not hear the words but will receive the channeled knowledge differently. A certain knowing will come to the surface, or a strong intuitive urge will be felt within. It is imperative to follow up on these urges or feelings.

Pictures, ideas, and thoughts will also be put into your head by one of your spirit guides or angels when you are linked together in this special meditative state.

The angels and guides above work through you in many ways, passing on knowledge, wisdom, teachings, and guidance. As stated before, healing energy will also be channeled through some practitioners.

The information, energy, and gifts that you receive from your angels and spirit guides can depend on the particular path you are on or at what vibrational level your aura, chakras, and physical body, are tuned.

When you feel that you have communicated with one of your spirit guides or angels long enough, then simply thank this entity with sincerity and let him or her leave your energy field as you think of this disconnection between both of you. Observe your face, your aura, and especially your crown chakra and the top of your head as this loving being ascends out of your energy field.

You might even notice another silhouette hovering above your head outside of your aura at this time. This is another guide or angel nearby, observing the event. You can have this loving being also enter into your energy and chakras to "channel" through you and communicate with you.

There are some individuals who are natural spirit mediums or channelers. Spirit guides, departed loved ones, and, in special cases, angels will work through them on a regular basis. Most of these people have been "channeling" or in close contact with the higher realms since early childhood. They are simply not aware of this as a gift and may consider themselves as having a mental illness or, at the very least, an overactive imagination; this is not the case. Hopefully, these people will recognize this ability and use it to help themselves and, most importantly, others.

In the recent past, some with clairvoyant or clairaudient abilities might have experienced psychiatric evaluation and been confined for observation in an institution by doctors or other experts who were unenlightened. After all, seeing things and hearing voices used to signal mental problems according to our society.

Once you have made the initial connection with one of your guides or angels using the Candle and Mirror Technique, Phase Three, you will become proficient at channeling. It will soon be a natural process, almost second nature to you.

Eventually, you will no longer need to use the Candle and Mirror Techniques at all. You will learn to feel the presence of these loving entities around you and ask for any of them to descend into your auric field and chakras. If you wish, you can still practice the Candle and Mirror Techniques for pleasure and experimentation, but at this stage they will no longer be necessary for channeling.

Incidentally, the pineal gland, the hypothalamus, and the pituitary gland play primary roles in the channeling process. These areas of the brain are linked to the crown and third eye chakras. The high vibratory energy of your spirit guides and angels will descend into the crown and third eye centers where it will be lowered or "stepped down" to a lower vibration, first by the pituitary gland, and then the pineal gland. Both these glands work in much the same fashion as step-down transformers in electronics; a certain frequency is changed or lowered to another frequency or vibration.

## Mutual Face Gazing Technique

This Face Gazing Technique is pleasant and enjoyable. Instead of using the Candle and Mirror Technique, find a partner or friend to practice face gazing. Ensure that the room is a near-dusk environment or is completely dark with only a few candles to light it, enough for you and your partner to see each other adequately.

Now, both of you should sit in comfortable positions facing each other, with about five feet of distance between you. Take a few deep breaths in and out, relaxing yourselves. Then start gazing through each other's eyes and faces in the same manner as you did in the Candle and Mirror Technique, Phase One.

In essence, you and your friend are substituting the mirror gazing with each other's faces. Simply do the same thing with each other's faces and auras as you did with all three phases of the Candle and Mirror Technique.

If you are successful, you will both see the silhouettes and sense the energies of each other's spirit guides and angels as you enter into deep altered states.

Continue gazing at each other's eyes, faces, and expanded auras for some time. Observe how you feel within and what you sense or see around both of you. The energy in the room should feel peaceful and pleasant. Finally, when you and your partner have experimented long enough, take in a deep breath and hold it for a few seconds, then release it slowly. Let yourselves come back to normal awareness.

A word of caution—make sure that the friend or partner you choose for the Mutual Face Gazing Technique is balanced, reasonably happy, and stable. A person with a lot of anger, sadness, and negativity inside can sometimes draw less than loving entities around him or her.

This enjoyable technique can be done whenever you wish, provided necessary precautions are taken to ensure that you, your partner, and the room itself have raised the proper vibrations for effective, safe channeling.

## Wall or Background Technique (Extension)

In chapter 5, "Reading and Interpreting the Human Aura," the Wall or Background Technique was given to you. Review this technique if you need to and then repeat it.

Once you have succeeded in seeing the aura above and around the head of your subject, look either above or off

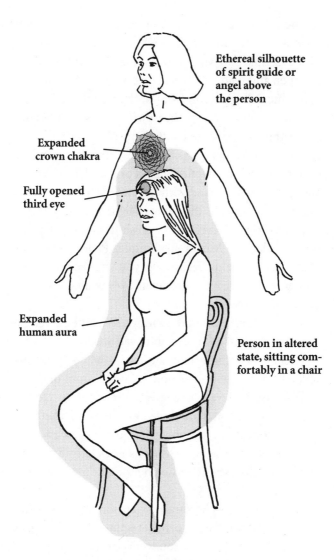

Ethereal silhouette
of spirit guide or
angel above
the person

Expanded
crown chakra

Fully opened
third eye

Expanded
human aura

Person in altered
state, sitting com-
fortably in a chair

Channeling Process—This illustration shows the spirit guide or
angel above a person's aura, ready to join with the individual.

to one side of him or her. The same type of silhouette or silhouettes that you noticed while practicing Phase Three of the Candle and Mirror Technique will appear when you are open and ready. A human-like shape of etheric white or light blue will appear in front of the wall or background.

You are now seeing the spirit guides or possibly the angels that are associated with your subject or friend. Watch as one of these beings (silhouettes) moves up and down, even into the human energy field of your friend. His or her energy field will expand with the crown chakra area becoming much brighter as the being of light settles within.

Just as you observed the facial shifts and overlays during the Candle and Mirror Technique, Phase One, and the Mutual Face Gazing Technique, you will see the same phenomenon occurring before your eyes while looking at the person sitting before you.

This phenomenon may continue to happen several more times as you watch the face and head areas.

Finally, have the person sitting in the chair against the wall take in a deep breath, hold it for the count of three, and then release it. Have your subject or friend return to normal consciousness. You should also do the same thing, letting yourself come back to a normal state of awareness.

If you want to switch positions now, letting your friend or subject observe the same phenomenon as you, feel free to try.

The Wall or Background Extension Technique should become part of your normal regimen for seeing auras, spirit guides, and angels. You will start to attune yourself to the higher energies of the heavenly fields and be able to link your earthly realm with the heavens above.

# The Many Reasons for Channeling

Channeling allows you access to the heavenly realms and God the Creator. Knowledge, wisdom, divine insight, and reassurance can come to all people through channeling, the connection with your spirit guides and angelic beings.

Special gifts can be yours when you work with these light beings that come down to earth. In fact, teaching, counseling, and healing are but three of the many gifts or abilities that many of you will gain as you awaken within and become channels.

Ideas, inventions, and solutions to numerous problems are given to many in order to benefit the world. Many answers and profound information become available to you as you learn to communicate effectively with spirit guides and angels and your intuitive and creative abilities become stronger. Even the potential for "super learning" will manifest itself in you as different areas of the brain are opened up.

Throughout history, creative individuals have "channeled" information from the heavenly fields and created masterpieces. Greek and Roman philosophers brought profound thoughts and uplifting ideas to the human masses through "channeled" writing. The Renaissance artist Michelangelo gazed into the sky one day and saw divine images being created in the white clouds floating above; his inspirational vision manifested in the beautiful artwork of the Sistine Chapel in Rome. Composers of classical music set their inspiration down and recorded the music of the spheres. Writers like Shakespeare and Voltaire brought forth words of wonder, as have many gifted poets whose words of love infused this realm with poetry.

This leads us to a greater realization: the channeling phenomenon has been present among us for thousands of years. It has always been a part of humankind, and will continue to be. In the future, this way of communicating with the higher realms will be even more profound and even commonplace; our present society is already showing evidence of this. More people are awakening to their true potential as multidimensional beings capable of working with both heavenly and earthly realms.

There are more individuals now who are spirit mediums than ever before. Perhaps, for some of you, the gift to talk with and see someone's departed relatives and friends will help you to comfort, reassure, and inspire the grieving ones left behind on the physical realm.

The finality of death becomes less real as you grow on your spiritual path. Working with your spirit guides and angels helps you to understand that death is but a transition to a higher level: the heavenly fields. The knowledge that you are part of the Creator, the heavens above, and the vibrational energy of the universe lets you place the process of birth and death into meaningful order.

Safe and proper channeling is one of the paths towards true enlightenment.

## Negative Channeling and Possession

Negative channeling refers to communication with beings, spirits, and entities that are from the dark side. These non-human essences do not possess any love or caring for the human "hosts" that are their prey. They sometimes will feel evil, chaotic, and uncomfortable when they are around a person.

If seen or sensed by a person, these unenlightened entities will appear dark and often misshapen. Some people who do not understand will mistake these grayish, dark-looking beings as spirit guides. *Do not be deceived!* Pay attention to what you see and how you feel when in the presence of someone who is being affected by these unheavenly creatures.

Teenagers and young people who are unhappy, sad, and emotionally mixed-up can be prime hosts for such negative entities. These young people possess many psychic abilities such as empathic skills and natural channeling attributes. Therefore, they will start to "channel" or connect with spirit entities that are either good or bad and be unaware of what is taking place. The negativity of these individuals lowers the vibratory rates of their auras, chakras, and bodies, thus attracting entities of a similar lower vibration.

Soon, these beings from the dark side will start to influence the thoughts and actions of these receptive teenagers and other young persons. Depression, suicidal thoughts, and other negative feelings will become stronger within the individuals as the negative spirits gain a greater hold upon them. Even the auric field of these people will develop a dirtier appearance.

There are four different degrees or phases associated with negative channeling (source: Dr. Winafred Blake Lucas, *Regression Therapy: A Handbook for Professionals, Volume II*, p. 358). They are as follows:

1. Shadowing occurs when the negative entity is outside a host, but is near to the host's aura and body, thus influencing the person intermittently or in a mild way.

2. Oppression happens when the negative spirit or entity is within the auric field of the person. The person will become affected emotionally in a perceptible but subtle way.

3. Obsession occurs when the negative being invades the physical body of its host, bringing with it all its own personality traits and habits, including some very bad and undesirable ones. The person being invaded will often be perplexed and confused because of this situation.

4. Possession happens when the invader (i.e., the negative entity) completely forces out the resident person's psyche and takes control of the physical body, through which it exhibits its own undesirable behaviors and speaks its own words. There may be transitions between possession and obsession at this point.

These four degrees of negative channeling are sometimes taught in parapsychology courses at universities featuring special disciplines. As well, both Anglican and Catholic priests comprehend this knowledge as part of their training.

How are negative entities to be avoided? The most important thing is to be fully aware of all aspects of the phenomena of channeling. Both the beneficial and less than beneficial characteristics should be known in order for you to stop fearing and worrying about the negative or dark side.

All the techniques discussed above will help to ensure that you *only* work with angels and guides as part of your lifelong spiritual quest.

If by chance a negative entity comes into your presence while in an altered state, you will instantly sense or know that it is of the dark side and possesses low vibrations full of negative impressions. You must tell it to leave at once because it is not "of the Creator and the Light." Ask for your angels and spirit guides to come to you for protection. Feel love and peace within. Soon the negative spirit will disperse and you may return to your meditation and channeling work.

## Neutral Spirits

Neutral spirits are simply lost souls and unenlightened entities that are in between the heavenly fields and the earthly realm. They are not harmful, only curious or needy. Many of them just wander between both realms.

## Spirit Boards

A brief mention should be made here regarding Ouija boards and spirit boards (the latter are merely a fancier version of the old standard Ouija boards). The use of either of these devices is a form of very primitive and elementary channeling procedures.

Nevertheless, a problem exists with these boards in that there is no "screening process" when playing with them or using them to contact spirits. It is much like having a party in your home, opening the front door, and inviting anyone and everyone in from the street. You have no control over the situation and will have no idea what to really expect. Both negative and positive entities can come to visit. The chances are that there will be more negative entities as well as neutral spirits within your home, particularly in the room where the Ouija or spirit board is being used.

In general such boards should be avoided. The only proper way to contact spirit guides or angels is through the correct techniques given throughout this book.

# Channeling and the Bible

There are many references of channeling recorded in the Bible, especially in the New Testament. All mentions made to the "Holy Ghost" or "Holy Spirit" throughout parts of this sacred text are direct examples of specific forms of channeling.

The writers of the Gospels either did not fully comprehend the channeling phenomenon, and therefore explained the events they witnessed as produced by the "Holy Ghost," or "Holy Spirit being upon them"; or else they expressed themselves in this manner in order to pass on hidden teachings to mystics and other spiritually awakened individuals who would come after them.

Many of these writings found in the New Testament are the true teachings of Jesus that have survived in their esoteric form. With an awakened third eye you will be able to recognize these words. Even given the centuries of censoring, editing, and purging of the true teachings of both the Ancient Mystery Schools and Jesus the Master Teacher, these teachings have survived in a special, covert form within the framework of the existing books of the Bible.

Whenever you read about the Holy Spirit in the Bible, try to remember that it is the high vibratory energy, the universal healing energy, the energy of the angels, and the Creator's love coming down from the heavenly fields through the eighth chakra and into the crown and third eye chakras of the person(s) open to receive this energy. These high energies will also work through all of the chakras, the bodies, the auras, and whole beings of individuals presenting them with great gifts.

Your angels and spirit guides are always with you, ready to assist you with your affairs. They will comfort, protect, and inspire you when needed. These beings of light and love will guide you in all your ways if you but give them a chance.

> Love and compassion are necessities, not luxu-
> ries. Without them humanity cannot survive . . .
> —Tenzin Gyatso (His Holiness
> the 14th Dalai Lama, born 1935)

# Chapter 9

## *Astral Projection*

Look within! The secret is inside you!
—Hui Neng (Chinese Buddhist
Leader, 638-713)

The art of astral travel or astral projection provides another way for you to meet your spirit guides and angels. When you take on your astral or soul form, you will be able to communicate more effectively with these light beings. They will teach and counsel you while you are in this state, a condition that allows you to be free of your physical body.

You will also be aware of the fact that these entities of love and light have a sense of humor. Through them, you will learn to take yourself less seriously and start to really live with all the foibles and fun this world can provide.

Astral travel, sleep, and death are all closely associated with one another; there is very little difference between these states. In all of them, your soul or true essence slips out of the physical form and begins to travel about your bedroom, then around your whole home (in certain cases), and finally to higher levels or higher vibrations.

The art of astral travel can be practiced while you are awake in an altered state, while you are in between sleep and waking state, or while you are in a deep sleep. Essentially, when you are sleeping, your soul leaves your body and auric field via either the solar plexus or crown chakras.

There are many examples of how this experience takes place in world spirituality. For example, in the beliefs of the Dakota (Sioux) Nation, the area at the top of the head allows the soul or part of the soul to leave from the body into the spirit world. Touching or patting the head of a Dakota child is sometimes frowned upon because this action may interfere with the comings and goings of the soul.

In certain other native groups of North America, tradition dictates that mourners wait four days before a deceased person is buried or cremated. To these groups, the number four is considered sacred and, in any case, the disposal of the physical body should not be performed before seventy-two hours have elapsed. This allows the human soul to completely disengage from the physical world and then travel with the assigned angels and spirit guides back up into the heavenly fields.

On the other side of the world, Tibetan Buddhists believe that the human soul leaves the body by way of the solar plexus chakra. As it lifts out of the aura, it maintains a connection with the body by a light or energy cord, referred to as "the silver cord." This special cord ensures that both the body and soul are still together; it is the silver cord that helps your soul to settle back into the physical form after soul traveling. At death, the silver cord disconnects from the physical body and stays attached to the human soul. This cord contains the vital life force or Universal Energy that is everywhere. It normally takes up to three days for the human soul along with the life force of the silver cord to completely dislodge from the body. In this tradition, it is usual to wait at least three days before the burial or cremation of the deceased, a comparable time to that observed by the Native Americans.

Most people can remember having dreams where you were flying or floating. This is recall of an astral dream or astral travel event, and is normal. You do this all the time while asleep, but are not aware of it in most situations.

During your astral travels, you will visit higher levels or planes of existence. Some of you will go to healing temples to have special healing work performed on you by angelic healers. Some will go to outdoor gardens and parks where spirit guides and certain angels operate as teachers, imparting knowledge and wisdom you need to bring back to earth when you awaken. Others of you will vibrate your souls to the level where the Akashic Records or Universal Library exist; it is here that you will access past and future life information, when you are ready. Information about other people can also be received here by you. It is as if this library holds "soul files" on everyone on earth. A librarian or scholarly spirit guide will assist you in this "higher place of learning."

In unique situations, you can perform astral travel for the purpose of healing others. This is a form of distance or absent healing whereby your soul leaves your body either during sleep or in a deep altered state and visits the bedside of a sick friend or relative.

While you are in your soul essence or astral body, you can place your hands onto the patient and send high vibratory healing energy to the afflicted area. You will have a healing angel or two, even three, accompany you if you ask for the help of angels in your thoughts. These healers will join their energies with you and assist in the treatment of the sick person. You and the angels will even penetrate the body into the internal organs with your "hands" and remove the diseased parts if necessary. This type of soul travel and healing is rare and requires the individual attempting it to be a very spiritually advanced person with developed psychic abilities.

Through training and practice, you can develop your healing gifts to this level. Many healers throughout history have used these techniques. In the Egyptian healing temples and ancient mystery schools, this rare type of astral travel was taught to more advanced students. Jesus and many of his disciples were also able to perform amazing feats of healing nearly 2,000 years ago. Medical Lamas of Tibet were also fully knowledgeable in this matter.

There are specific techniques that you can do for the direct purpose of astral projection.

## Glass of Water Technique

In chapter 6, "The Chakra System," an exercise was presented for the opening of the palm or hand chakras. The Hand Chakra Opening Technique can be performed again as a warmup at this time. Review the technique if necessary. Once you have "opened" the hand chakras up and increased healing energy into the whole hand, you are ready for the next technique. It is a natural progression to follow.

Fill an average size glass with water in preparation for this technique.

Upon completing the Hand Chakra Opening Technique, pick up the glass of water and hold it between both of your hands. Your hands, palms, and fingers are now all open, warmed up and alive with natural healing energy. This healing exercise contains the vital life force that exists within the human body. It is ready to be released from the palm chakras, thumbs, index, and middle fingers.

By placing your hands around the glass in a comfortable position keeping sufficient contact with the surface of the glass, you allow the vital life force or *chi* to enter the glass and be absorbed by the water. Remember that the right hand possesses the positive essence of this vital life force and the left hand has the negative essence of this energy. Under the law of magnetism, like repels like and like attracts unlike. The positive essence of the right hand attracts the negative essence of the left hand. Both of these polarities combine as one in the glass of water. In reality, the glass of water will eventually become charged or magnetized with this *chi* as you hold it between your hands.

While you hold the glass, continue to focus your attention on the palms and fingers of the hands and glance into the water. Feel the pulsing in the hands getting stronger and stronger until it feels like a throbbing or "heart" beating that now is emanating from the glass of water. Keep all your attention on the hands pulsing and the water between them beginning to "feel" different.

After about five to ten minutes of this attention focusing and sending energy into the water you will be able to sense that the water is charged or magnetized. It might even feel as if the glass is trying to push your hands away from it.

If the room that you are sitting in has a low light level or a near-dusk environment, you will notice a light blue type of energy either within the water or surrounding the glass and your hands in some cases.

Now, take the glass of water and drink it all down quickly. In a few moments you might start to feel a warm sensation in the pit of your stomach, or perhaps a sense of relaxation settling through you. This is part of the desired effect. This charged water that contains the life force or energy is working through your system now regenerating your cells, blood, tissue, and essentially all of you. This water works as a tonic on your whole system, relaxing and revitalizing you at the same time. More positive energy is absorbed into your body by performing the Glass of Water Technique.

The human body and the soul also function under the law of magnetism. The body is normally operating with negative energy; while the human soul operates with a more positive energy. This arrangement keeps the soul and body connected to one another because positive attracts negative.

This special technique changes the polarity of the body, making it more positive. When this happens it becomes easier to try astral projection. This is because the now more positive body begins to repel the positive soul and, as a result, the soul can slip out of the body with less difficulty.

The Glass of Water Technique can be performed prior to attempting astral travel in an altered state or going to sleep. If you perform the water exercise just before lying down and going to sleep, you will have one of following experiences.

You might, if very fortunate, project yourself astrally out of your body and float about the room while in an altered or relaxed waking state. It is more likely that you will have your soul with all your awareness slip out of the physical form while you are in between the waking and sleeping state, or when you fall into sleep.

If you project yourself astrally while either in the in-between condition or the sleeping condition,  you will be fully aware of the event taking place. You will experience and recall everything during these two states of consciousness. Therefore, the Glass of Water Technique helps you to remember your flying dreams or astral travel upon awakening.

There is one final thing to mention about this technique and astral travel in general. While lying or sitting, before you enter into an altered state or drift off to sleep, you may experience specific physiological sensations within. Sometimes you feel that you are vibrating either back and forth or up and down in your body. This is because your soul is already starting to shift out of the physical form. Or, you might feel that you are lifting out of your body and attempting to move towards the ceiling above. Again, this is because the soul is less encumbered.

## Breath Holding Technique

This breathing technique should be performed just after the Glass of Water Technique and should be considered an important part of the whole process for astral projection.

While you are either sitting comfortably or lying down, start to take in a few normal breaths. Now, take in another breath and hold it for as long as you can and feel the air in your lungs trying to burst forth. Feel the pressure in the chest and then finally release this pent-up breath slowly out of your mouth.

Practice this breath holding exercise a second time, and then a third and final time.

During the final time, a variation should be done when you release the breath out of your mouth. This time expel the breath quickly and feel that you are forcing yourself from your body. Focus on a spot in front of you, if you are sitting, or above you if you are lying down, and picture yourself there looking back at your physical body.

If you are successful, you will slip out of your body and gaze back at your physical form while in the astral state of existence. If not, let yourself get into a deeper state of meditation or just drift off to sleep. In any case, you will begin to have your soul leave the body while meditating or, if asleep, you will have a total recall of the astral projection upon returning to a waking state. Sometimes, you will achieve the in-between waking and sleeping state and enjoy your astral journey. Eventually, you will become more proficient at this and start to visit the higher levels associated with the heavenly fields.

The Breath Holding Technique is very important for astral travel due to the fact that Universal Energy, vital life force, and higher vibrations of energy that are in the air are drawn into your lungs. By holding your breath as long as is possible comfortably, you let these energies work through the blood stream, heart, and essentially all your body. This increases the positive energy in the body to an even higher degree and thus makes it even easier for your soul to slip out.

It is recommended that you perform the Glass of Water Technique and the Breath Holding Technique in conjunction with one another. This will ensure greater success for you in the future.

The more you practice this method of astral projection experimentation, the more proficient you will become. This ability will open up new opportunities for you and allow you to explore new worlds.

> Canst thou think too greatly of thy Soul? Or can too much be said in its praise? It is the essence of Him who gave it.
> —*Unto Thee I Grant*

# Chapter 10

## *Reincarnation*

Yea, I am one with all I see,
With wind and wave, with pine and palm;
Their very elements in me
are fused to make me what I am.
Through me their common life-stream flows,
And when I yield this human breath,
In leaf and blossom, bud and rose,
Live on I will . . . There is no death!
—Robert Service (poet, 1874–1958)

To be born into a physical body, to live and die, and then to be reborn into another physical form: this is the central concept of reincarnation. The belief in this process of transformation is fast becoming a part of the culture of Western society as more people awaken within themselves. The theory of reincarnation has already been accepted as reality in Eastern society for thousands of years; in fact, it forms the core belief in both Hinduism and Buddhism. This is one of the reasons why many people in Western countries are now embracing Buddhism.

Reincarnation answers many questions that pertain to your reason for being here on earth. It helps you put your life into proper perspective and gives you a better understanding of the cycle of life and death.

Most of you believe that you have an immortal soul that enters the physical body at the time of birth, and that the soul resides in this material form during your lifetime. At the moment of death, that very soul, your soul, then leaves the body (its "shell") and journeys back to heaven. If you accept this concept readily, why not the concept of reincarnation? After all, if the immortal soul can come down to earth and join with a physical body once, why not a second time?

In the days of Jesus the Master Teacher, reincarnation was considered common knowledge; it was accepted as part of life. The original teachings of Jesus also involved the theory of reincarnation. Unfortunately, many of these references to reincarnation by Jesus and other great spiritual teachers were carefully deleted from many ancient texts that were considered part of the Bible.

Most of the bishops and leaders of the early, but rapidly growing Christian Church removed several books from this sacred literature in the hopes of removing any or all references to reincarnation (at the Council of Nicaea, 325 C.E.) These men were striving for power, and they wanted to control the population and ultimately the known world of the time (i.e., the Roman Empire). By eliminating the idea of birth to rebirth from their doctrine, replacing it instead with the idea of only one lifetime per person followed by either eternal hell or heaven depending on the person's actions, their beliefs created a greater need for the Christian Church as an institution for salvation from death.

This untrue concept of heaven and hell has been lessening its grip on people as they seek a true spiritual path, discovering on their journey the real teachings of Jesus and the ancient teachings of the mystery schools.

Despite the early Church's attempt at censoring, there are some specific references to reincarnation still found within the pages of the present Bible. In the New Testament (specifically, the Book of Matthew), an intimation is made to Jesus Christ as the returning prophet, Elijah. In the Old Testament, references to reincarnation can be found in Exodus 20:4 and Psalms 90:3.

In chapter 9, the real dynamics of the Holy Ghost or Holy Spirit were explained. Also, mystical wisdoms and esoterically hidden messages were described as they appear within the words of the Bible. The mention of the Holy Spirit or Holy Ghost itself in the Bible has a connection to the theory of reincarnation. When early Christianity borrowed the doctrine of the Holy Trinity from teachings derived from ancient Hinduism, it also created a hidden, mystical message in this idea.

The ancient mystery schools and healing temples taught the Law of Three or the Law of the Triangle to its students for many centuries. This law taught that three things or "essences" were required to create or manifest something such as life.

Jesus also taught this to his many disciples, both male and female, during his lifetime. This Law of Three was a reference to the theory of reincarnation. Many of his followers eventually put this teaching into their writings.

The early Christian fathers—the more enlightened ones—blended the Holy Trinity of Hinduism with the Law of the Triangle from the teachings of Jesus, creating the

## The Law of Three

| Father | Son | Holy Spirit | Heaven |
|--------|-----|-------------|--------|
| ┊ | ┊ | ┊ | |
| Soul | Body | Universal | Earth |

## The Law of the Triangle

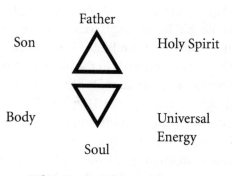

Father

Son

Holy Spirit

Body

Universal
Energy

Soul

## The Star of David

This symbol
represents heaven
and earth

The Law of Three, the Law of the Triangle, and the Star of
David.

Holy Trinity that Christianity now recognizes. The Father, the Son, the Holy Spirit refer to the soul, the body, and the Universal Energy or life force.

As was mentioned in chapter 9, the immortal soul enters the physical body at or before birth and that spirit energy, life force, or Universal Energy is needed to help keep both body and soul connected. This energy works like a magnet, maintaining the human soul within the physical form. Three essences are needed to manifest life: soul, body, and life force.

The same principle holds true at the time of death. As a person dies, the life force leaves the body and its quickly depleting aura, returning to the universe. When this energy leaves, the immortal soul cannot keep itself within the body, and journeys back to the heavenly fields shortly afterwards. Death has now occurred. This process repeats itself over and over until you eventually break the reincarnation cycle and return to the heavenly realms permanently.

> The words of the great teachers and guides of
> humanity are streams of power and light.
> —Mouni Sadhu (mystic and
> guru, twentieth century)

There are two conditions that can affect this cycle of life and death in reincarnation. These conditions are called karma and dharma.

As used in Buddhism and Hinduism, karma refers to the actions taken by someone during a particular lifetime. These actions, either good or bad, will sometimes determine that person's destiny in a present incarnation sometimes, and always in future incarnations. According to this belief, if you were cruel and abusive to your spouse in a previous lifetime, you would return in a future one and possibly experience the roles in reverse, whereby your spouse would now be abusive towards you. Many people believe that if you are suffering hardship and trouble in this life it is because of your actions from a past incarnation.

Recognizing this karma or karmic debt in your present lifetime and then changing your patterns now will result in a release of this debt. In essence, you will then start to break the cycle of birth to rebirth because you have learned your lesson. This is part of your spiritual growth or evolution. The quicker you break or release these karmic debts, the quicker your soul growth and your return to the heavenly fields where you will remain.

Dharma, on the other hand, is just the opposite of karma. It specifically involves good thoughts and good actions. People who help and dedicate their lives in service to humanity are creating dharma or "scoring points in heaven."

Love and kindness shown to others will help you to break the cycle of reincarnation much faster than if you simply went through life doing nothing at all, simply coasting through this incarnation.

Dharma also represents a great cleansing "to wipe the slate clean," as they say. Karmic debt loads can be eliminated in a very short time when you help others unselfishly. Your motives should be pure and good.

Always be aware of your thoughts and actions and try not to judge others too harshly. Create thoughts of love and peace in your heart and mind. This will aid you in your spiritual growth, allowing you to become a better person and a kinder human soul.

## The Many Reasons for Past Life Regression

The veil that comes down on you during the traumatic process of being born, causing you to forget your past incarnations, can be lifted through past life regression.

There are many reasons to delve into the past,  exploring your previous lives.

- Emotional Healing. Anger, sadness, grief, hatred, and other negative emotions created by past life events and sufferings can be brought up to the surface of your conscious mind and be released safely. A permanent healing can then occur.

- Physical Healing. Unexplained pains and health issues that plague you and cannot be healed through conventional medicine can be traced in many cases to previous incarnations. By "re-living" the accident or death scene, you can bring the memory of the pain to the consciousness of your mind and thereby release the pain. A profound healing of longstanding problems may then take place.

- Release of Fears and Phobias. Unexplained fears and unfounded phobias can be remembered through past life recall, brought to the surface of the conscious mind, analyzed, and released quickly. Soon, a fear or phobia that hounded you for many years will no longer exist, or at least not affect you as much.

- Understanding and Healing of Relationship Problems. The recall of a past life relationship with someone that you are involved with now will help you to recognize negative patterns in the relationship, allowing you to break or heal these patterns. You will understand where love-hate relationships originate.

- Receiving of Gifts and Attributes. By exploring a past life, you will not only recall that incarnation but also in some situations remember or relearn certain gifts and attributes. For example, if you were a healer using herbs in an earlier lifetime, you will be able to reawaken some of your knowledge of herbs. This is a form of super learning.

Throughout this book, you have been presented with detailed techniques and exercises for the purpose of developing your psychic abilities and spiritual growth. Some of these exercises have also been designed to be used for past life recall.

The Candle and Mirror Technique, Phase One, is a prime example. Use this technique as often as you wish when exploring your past lives.

Both guided meditation and hypnotherapy are very effective methods for lifting the veil placed upon you at birth, thus allowing you to recall past incarnations. The use of specially designed guided meditation tapes may aid many of you as well.

The knowledge that you are eternal and are the composite of all your previous lifetimes allows you to understand who you truly are, why you are here on planet earth, and where you are going after experiencing this realm of existence.

> Jesus said, "I disclose my mysteries to those who are worthy of my mysteries."
> —The sayings of Jesus Christ

# Chapter 11

# *The Master's Last Days*

He rises like the palm tree in spite of oppression; and as an eagle in the firmament of heaven he soars aloft, and fixes his eyes upon the glories of the sun.
—*Unto Thee I Grant*

In this book, the secrets and esoteric knowledge of the ancient mystery schools have been passed on to you, the student. These same teachings were instilled in the Master Jesus by this system nearly 2,000 years ago, when he attended various centers and schools of metaphysical studies. The education of the Master Jesus was touched on in chapter 1. Here, we will explore the life and learning of this fascinating man in more detail.

During his lifetime, Jesus taught his many disciples, both male and female, the very same mysteries and philosophical beliefs discussed in these pages. These spiritual and psychic principles were given to his followers, who in turn passed them on to others. The pages of the New Testament record some of these esoteric messages in subtle ways, sometimes in the form of parables and the descriptions of miracles. Some of the wisdom that Jesus taught was hidden in the gospels found in the Bible. Unfortunately, the majority of his teachings were suppressed or removed from the reach of the general public by those later Christian officials who compiled the texts of the New Testament.

The Gnostic Gospels, a collection of biblical writings found in the twentieth century near Nag Hammadi, Egypt, contain some of this knowledge, as well as pertinent information about the life of Jesus. He was a real historical person who lived, laughed, loved, cried, and suffered just like everyone else.

Due to the fact that this book is based on the teachings of the Ancient Mystery Schools as taught by the Master Jesus, it becomes essential to understand more about this wonderful man and teacher, not as a godlike being, but as a highly evolved human with a special purpose for mankind.

As a man, Jesus had normal wants and feelings regarding love and sex. A reference to this fact is clearly made in the Gospel of Philip, one of the original texts found preserved at Nag Hammadi (quoted from Pagels, *The Gnostic Gospels*):

> . . . the companion of the Savior is Mary Magdalene. But Christ loved her more than all the disciples and used to kiss her often on her mouth. The rest of the disciples were offended by it . . . They said to him, "Why do you love her more than all of us?" The Savior answered and said to them, "Why do I not love you as I love her?"

The traditional, "recognized" Gospels of Matthew, Mark, Luke, and John show Jesus appearing in many places during his short ministry. This might lead some readers of the stories to believe that he was everywhere, or perhaps that he had a lookalike assisting him with his ministry.

If this is indeed true, certain questions and theories might arise. The birth of the Master Jesus and even his death could take on different ramifications.

In one of the Gnostic Gospels, a twin brother to Jesus is mentioned. The Gospel of Thomas, which is believed by many scholars to be the actual words of the Master recorded in his lifetime, makes a particularly startling statement (ibid.):

> These are the secret words which the living Jesus spoke, and which the twin, Judas Thomas, wrote down.

By placing these examples of written, literary evidence into this chapter, the following discussion may be taken in context and become more plausible for you, the reader and student, to consider.

Chapters 2 through 10 contain a step-by-step approach to psychic and spiritual development. The world around you will become more wondrous when you can see auras, chakras, spirit guides, and angels. Working with your guides and angels, while either asleep or in an altered state of waking, will allow you access to amazing information that can be helpful to yourself and others. The recollection of past lives can open even more doors for you, giving you insight, information, and attributes into the secret workings behind the waking world. The ability to raise your vibrations will enable you to travel astrally to higher levels of the heavenly fields, where you can visit teaching temples and the Akashic Records themselves. From these sources, you can gain access to wisdom and knowledge pertaining to yourself and those around you.

The author of this book has developed the abilities mentioned above, and he now uses them to assist others on their path. A vivid remembrance of a past life at the time of Jesus, as well as nightly visits to the Akashic Records, have allowed the following dialogue to be brought forth.

Please keep an open mind as you read this particularly important conversation between Jesus and a disciple.

## The Deathbed of Jesus

Jesus the Master Teacher lay on his deathbed in a secluded bedroom at the Essene Mystery School of Mount Carmel. It was the second year of the reign of the Roman Emperor Trajan. The Master was rumored to be almost 109 years of age.

From Mount Carmel, Jesus had overseen his organization and advised his many disciples over a period of almost seven decades.

Matthias, the grandson of Matthew, the former tax collector and disciple, sat in a chair beside the bed of Jesus. A sad smile lay upon his young bearded face as he gazed at the ancient face of Jesus. The beautiful blue eyes of the Master looked back at him. Those eyes were still as bright and penetrating as ever.

"Matthias, my young friend and disciple, try not to be so sad," Jesus smiled and laughed. "After all, everything of this earth has its own cycle. Death is merely a continuation of life in a higher form."

"But Master," exclaimed Matthias in an anguished voice, "we will miss you dearly."

"Remember what I taught you, Matthias. There is no death. There never will be. Our human souls are eternal and directly linked with God. It is the physical body that we reside in temporarily while we are here on earth that dies. We are souls with bodies, not the other way around. When our physical form can no longer house our soul, we vacate the house and vibrate to a higher energy and return to the heavenly fields. While up there, we rest, review that life, and receive special instructions. When we are ready, we return to earth where our soul enters into the body of a soon-to-be born child. We repeat this process again and again until we learn all our lessons here on the physical plane of existence." Jesus lifted his right hand and placed it on top of his young disciples' tightly clenched hands.

"Do not worry. We will all be together again in heaven and on earth in future lifetimes."

Matthias seemed to gain strength from these words. He unclenched his hands and gently squeezed the Master's hand in his and then sat back in the chair. He placed his hands in his lap. "You have asked me here. I came as soon as I received the message."

"Yes, I am pleased that you are here. My time is very limited and I must discuss certain concerns with you of events of the past. The manuscript that your grandfather Matthew wrote just prior to his passing is wonderful but it is not enough."

Jesus had to hold back tears as he thought of his close friend and disciple of many years. "You must realize that my teachings are based on ancient teachings from Atlantis and Egypt and are to be used as a spiritual way of life. It is not a religion and should never become one. I hold great fears regarding this!"

The young man looked down at the Master in a knowing way. Matthias started to think about the changes that had happened in his own lifetime. He knew Jesus' fears were not unfounded. "I know that you are speaking of Paul of Tarsus and others that have perverted the true teachings in the past."

The Master's still handsome face wrinkled up into a grimace as he replied, "Paul irked me greatly. He twisted my teachings and my sermons. He had a dislike of women and relegated them to secondary positions whenever he could. He influenced many men in key offices to turn my organization into a patriarchal system. The teachings, the words should have been spread by both women and men. Many of my own disciples have been women. God or the Creator is a supreme being consisting of both male and female principles. Both energies are necessary to manifest life."

Jesus shut his eyes for a few moments and focused on his breathing. His life energy was slipping fast. He opened his eyes again and continued, "I want you to record this and the following story I am about to relate to you. Your memory is excellent, Matthias, so you can simply listen to my tale now. Later, after I have passed on you can put my words into writing."

Matthias leaned forward in his chair giving the Master his full attention.

Jesus took in a deep but hesitant breath into his struggling lungs and began, "I wish to discuss the so-called crucifixion and resurrection. I feel somewhat burdened by it all."

His young disciple raised his eyebrows in surprise. "Why would you feel burdened by this miraculous event?"

The Master Teacher raised his right hand with effort motioning his young friend to silence.

"When I was forty years old and into my fourth year of teaching and administering, a dangerous situation arose. The Great Sanhedrin* and other powerful men were jealous of my influence on the populace. These men wanted me dead and sent spies to watch my every move. A conspiracy was formed to maneuver myself and my inner circle of twelve disciples into Jerusalem at Passover. Their intent was to have me arrested and tried for blasphemy. My crucifixion would have been the result."

"Joseph of Arimathea, a member of the Sanhedrin, was a sympathetic friend to our teachings. With great risk to his own life, he met me secretively near the village of Bethany and warned me of this conspiracy."

"All of us, including your grandfather Matthew, sat up late into the night and discussed our options. We were gathered in a circle by a grove of olive trees with a small fire in the center. It was Matthew in fact who came up with the solution to our grave problem. He suggested that my twin brother, Judah, could help us. The only discernible difference was that Judah had brown eyes not blue eyes."

Jesus stopped talking and gasped for breath a few times. His eyes were shut and his faced looked contorted. Finally, he regained his composure. "Anyway, it was decided to use Judah as my impersonator for awhile, as he had done in the past. My brother with the same spiritual persuasion as myself was approached with the idea. He wholeheartedly agreed to help us. Unfortunately, the plan went awry during the Passover.

"It was my twin who was arrested in the garden of Gethsemane on that night so long ago. Poor Judas Iscariat in

* The ecclesiastical and judicial court of ancient Judaea.

fear of his own life identified Judah as the Master with a kiss upon his cheek. When Judah, who was believed to be myself went before Pontius Pilatus, the procurator reluctantly condemned him. Pilatus was not fond of the Jews and was tolerant of my teachings. He did order his Roman soldiers not to break the legs of Judah in hopes of removing the man from the cross before death set in. This Roman official may have been cruel to some but for some reason he had a certain respect for the gentle Essenes and their way of life."

"When Judah was crucified in my place that day, there was a minor earthquake and a terrible rainstorm that arose. While this horrible event was unfolding, both Nicodemus, a disciple of our group, and Joseph of Arimathea approached Pontius Pilatus in private and begged the release of their Master from the cross. Pilatus quickly assented to their request and passed a hastily prepared order of reprieve to these two men."

Due to the powerful storm and the earthquake, very few people were left at the site of the crucifixion. Some of my followers, my mother and Mary of Magdala were present. A Roman centurion who was sympathetic to us was standing nearby the cross. Nicodemus thrust the document into the centurion's hands. From that point, all present removed poor Judah from his cross, wrapped him in linen and carried him away to the Essene healing grottoes nearby. Judah was still alive at this time. The Roman centurion remained at his post. He told any curious onlookers that came by later that Jesus was dead and had been taken away to be buried in a cave belonging to Joseph of Arimathea."

Matthias sat back in his chair and gasped in awe at Jesus. The small room was silent for several seconds. Only the occasional sound of birds and the wind blowing gently through the trees outside the bedroom window could be heard.

The Master Jesus commenced with his story again. "Sadly, my brave brother Judah did not recover from his ordeal. Pontius Pilatus sent Roman soldiers to the burial cave owned by Joseph of Arimathea. People were kept away from the area for three whole days. Finally, on the third day, after my so-called death, Mary of Magdala and some others who were privy to the secret, arrived at the burial cave. The Roman guards had already rolled back the huge boulder the previous night exposing an empty tomb. Mary of Magdala and the rest of them went out into the public proclaiming that Jesus had risen from the dead. Soon, word spread throughout the land, much to the consternation of certain members of the Great Sanhedrin."

Jesus started to gasp for air again, curtailing his amazing story. He shut his blue eyes and lay there struggling for life giving breath to enter his lungs.

Matthias turned his attention away from the face of Jesus and gazed out the window at the stone wall that encircled the huge complex. He watched as a black bird descended and landed on top of the wall. He started to search his memory wondering what a black bird meant.

Using his great clairvoyant ability, Jesus, who could not see behind him, spoke up. "Matthias, they say the sighting of a black bird foretells of death. Upon that wall sits a sign. It is my omen. When it flies away, my soul shall fly away also."

Darkness was starting to descend upon Jesus. With a final effort he spoke.

"I miss my beloved Mary of Magdala and all our children and grandchildren. All my old friends and disciples have long since gone. I feel sad and alone. I have lived, loved, and cried. My old body feels like a grain of sand upon the desert floor. With the coming of the wind, I will vanish from the land into the distance." A single tear rolled down his cheek. His eyes had a faraway look. "Promise me, Matthias, to record all of what I have said."

He closed his eyes and murmured, "Mary, I loved you so. How I missed you. It is time for me to go." Jesus let out one final breath and his body went still.

Suddenly, a beautiful white light appeared at the foot of his bed and soon the shape of an angel formed from this great light. At the same time, a white light arose from the body of Jesus known as the Christ and moved towards the beautiful angel. The heavenly messenger who appeared as a male started to shimmer and turned once more into a magnificent white light and became smaller. Both these illuminations moved about the room together and then exited through the bedroom window heading towards the black bird perched on top of the wall.

Matthias, the grandson of Matthew the former tax collector and disciple, gazed out the window at the apparition of death. Two swirls of white light danced together and moved towards the black bird. The bird flapped its ebony colored wings and lifted up into the sky. The brilliant white lights joined it in its ascent. All continued to gain height climbing towards the heavens. Soon the wondrous spectacle was lost to Matthias' eyes. The black bird of death along with its special companions had flown into the heavenly fields.

The soul of the Master Jesus had come home.

> Come to me, O troubled child.
> Come to me so meek and mild.
> When your eyes are full of tears,
> And your heart is full of fears.
> For I shall dry your tearful eyes.
> And I shall calm your fearful cries.
> —Douglas De Long

**Good Journey to You All!**

# Appendix 1

# *Illustrations and Charts*

**Chapter 1**
View of the Sphinx on the Giza Plateau, Egypt . . . . . . .6

**Chapter 2**
Diagram of brain with pineal, pituitary,
and hypothalamus . . . . . . . . . . . . . . . . . . . . . . . . . . . .26

Position of the third eye chakra . . . . . . . . . . . . . . . . . . .28

The Third Eye Exercise . . . . . . . . . . . . . . . . . . . . . . . .33

**Chapter 3**
Brain with pituitary and position
of crown chakra . . . . . . . . . . . . . . . . . . . . . . . . . . . . .38

Location of pituitary, hypothalamus, and pineal . . . . .39

Universal Energy Spectrum Phenomena . . . . . . . . . . .43

**Chapter 5**
Aura around a woman . . . . . . . . . . . . . . . . . . . . . . . . .83

Aura around head and shoulders . . . . . . . . . . . . . . . .93

**Chapter 6**
Chakras, their names, colors, and associated
Glands . . . . . . . . . . . . . . . . . . . . . . . . . . . . . . . . . . . . .98

Location of major chakras . . . . . . . . . . . . . . . . . . . . . .99

Energy meridians in a body . . . . . . . . . . . . . . . . . . . .104

Hand Warming Exercise . . . . . . . . . . . . . . . . . . . . . . . .106

Hand Circling  . . . . . . . . . . . . . . . . . . . . . . . . . . . . . . .111

**Chapter 7**
Chakra system, nervous system,
and kundalini  . . . . . . . . . . . . . . . . . . . . . . . . . . . . . . .139

**Chapter 8**
Channeling process . . . . . . . . . . . . . . . . . . . . . . . . . . . .191

**Chapter 10**
The Law of Three, the Law of the Triangle,
and the Star of David  . . . . . . . . . . . . . . . . . . . . . . . . . .214

# Appendix 2

# *The Colors of the Human Aura, Their Meaning, and Location*

A chart on the auric colors is provided for you on the following pages. This should give you a quick and easy reference to these energies and their meanings.

Because everyone sees the world differently, some people may see these amazing colors in a slightly different way than others. Perhaps one person will see a lighter shade of green than a friend does—this is normal.

Please consult chapter 4 for more detailed descriptions of the colors and their characteristics.

**Positive Colors**
> Light Blue, Mid Blue, Dark Blue, Light to Mid Green, Sunshine or Light Yellow, Baby Pink, Medium to Dark Red (Burgundy)

**Neutral Colors**
> Honey or Golden Brown

**Rare Positive Colors**
> White, Gold, Silver, Light Purple, Mid Purple (Indigo), Light to Mid Orange

**Negative Colors**
> Black, Gray, Dirty Yellow, Dirty Orange, Dirty/Dull Brown, Bright Pink, Light Red, Reddish Purple, Dark Green

| Colors | Meaning ("kind of person") | Location Listed Below |
|---|---|---|
| Positive Colors | Good, Beneficial Luminations | |
| Light Blue | A gentle, peaceful, and spiritual person | Around head area—½" to 6" from surface |
| Mid Blue | A technical, logical, and business-minded person | Around head area—2½" to 7" from surface |
| Dark Blue | An artistic, creative person | Around head area—4" to 10" from surface |
| Light to Mid Green | A person who is a natural healer, or possibly someone being healed | Surrounds head area, covers hair, and runs down the arms and hands |
| Sunshine or Light Yellow | A positive, outgoing person with high energy level | Around head area—1" to 4" from surface |
| Baby Pink | A person full of universal love for others | Around head area—8" to 14" from surface |
| Medium to Dark Red (Burgundy) | A sexually charged or lusty person (sometimes a person who is sexually frustrated) | Small clouds of energy around head area (sometimes present in other body areas) |
| Neutral Colors | A Lumination That is Neither Good Nor Bad | |
| Honey or Golden Brown | A person interested in wealth, power, and social position | Completely covers head area—1" to 3" from surface |

| Rare Positive Colors | Special Luminations Showing Psychic and Spiritual Enlightenment | Mostly Around Head Area of Aura (Exceptions Explained Below) |
|---|---|---|
| **White Pure Energy** | A person who is on a path or purpose in life; a more enlightened person | Surrounds head and eventually whole body |
| **Gold** | A person accessing universal wisdom and spiritual knowledge | Ranges from 6" to 8" above head to complete coverage of head |
| **Silver** | A person who is just starting on a path of purpose in life, becoming more awakened | Around head—1" to 3" from surface |
| **Light Purple** | A person using psychic gifts or abilities in a spiritual way | Crown chakra (top of head) and third eye chakra (forehead) |
| **Mid Purple (Indigo)** | A psychically awakened person | Crown chakra (top of head) and third eye chakra (forehead) |
| **Light to Mid Orange** | A person with a creative sense of humor | 8" to 10" above the head |

| Colors | Meaning ("kind of person") | Location |
|---|---|---|
| Negative Colors | Bad, Undesirable Luminations | As Listed Below |
| Black | A tired person lacking energy, or an unhappy and deceitful person | Either around head area or covering face |
| Gray | A sick person, possibly suffering from a headache or lack of energy; may also be abused | Either around head area or covering face |
| Dirty Yellow | A person with a physical illness or injury | Above the body area affected or injured |
| Dirty Orange | A very sick person, possibly suffering from cancer | Above and surrounding the affected area |
| Dirty/Dull Brown | Either a person in the late stages of dying, or someone with a very negative character (depends on the shade of brown) | Either surrounding the afflicted area or covering the body |
| Bright Pink | An extremely argumentative person | Around head area—3" to 6" from surface |
| Light Red | An angry person or one with an energy block in the body | Around side of head—fluctuates out from surface |
| Reddish Purple | An angry person with psychic abilities | Above crown chakra (top of head) or in third eye area (forehead) |
| Dark Kelly Green | An envious or jealous person who covets what others possess | Surrounding all or part of the head—4" to 7" from surface |

# Appendix 3

# *Index of Techniques, Exercises, and Meditations*

Aura Reading, 91

Baby, 118

Base Chakra Opening, 135

Breathing, 81

Breath Focusing, 117

Breath Holding, 207

Candle and Mirror—Phase One, 86

Candle and Mirror —Phase Two, 87

Candle and Mirror (Extension)—Phase One, 180

Candle and Mirror (Extension)—Phase Two, 185

Candle and Mirror (Extension)—Phase Three, 185

Candle Gazing, 89

Chanelling, 179

Crown Chakra Exercise, 44

Crown Chakra Opening, 145

Crown to Base Energy Flow, 154

Crown to Heart Energy Flow, 148

Glass of Water, 204

Hand Chakra Opening (Hand Warming), 102

Hand Circling, 131

Heart Chakra Opening, 115

Heart Chakra—Warmth Opening Flower, 147

Heart to Base Energy Flow, 151

Kundalini Arousal and Flow, 143

Loved One, 119

Mutual Face Gazing, 189

Palm Circling, 109

Puppy or Kitten, 122

Solar Plexus Opening, 128

Sacral Plexus Opening, 132

Raising the Vibrations of Your
    Environment, 172

Raising Your Vibrations, 177

Sunset Gazing, 90

The Third Eye, 30

Throat Chakra Opening, 109

Thyroid Stimulation, 110

Thumb and Finger, 107

Toning, 80

Tree Gazing, 85

Wall or Background, 82

Wall or Background (Exten-
    sion), 190

Warmth Opening Flower, 123

White Light Meditation, 179

# Endnotes

## *Works Quoted in Epigrams*

p. 1    Sri Ramatherin, ed. *Unto Thee I Grant.* 32nd ed. San Jose, Calif.: AMORC, 1979.

p. 23   Petras, Kathryn, and Ross Petras. *The Whole World Book of Quotations: Wisdom from Women and Men around the Globe Throughout the Centuries.* New York: Addison-Wesley, 1995.

p. 37   Cihlar, Many. *Mystics at Prayer.* 19th ed. San Jose, Calif.: The Rosicrucian Press Ltd., 1982.

p. 40   *The Whole World Book of Quotations.*

p. 51   *Holy Bible* (King James translation).

p. 91   Eliot, Charles W., ed. *The Meditations of Marcus Aurelius.* Danbury, Conn.: The Harvard Classics, Grolier Enterprises Corp, 1980.

p. 96   *The Whole World Book of Quotations.*

p. 115  Ibid.

p. 136  *The Golden Sayings of Epictetus.* Danbury, Conn.: Grolier Enterprises Corp, 1980.

p. 137  *The Whole World Book of Quotations.*

p. 147  Pagels, Elaine. *The Gnostic Gospels.* New York: Vintage Books, 1981.

p. 160    Plato. *Dialogues of Plato.* (*Timaeus* and *Critias*). New York: Penguin Books, 1986.

p. 161    *Holy Bible.*

p. 167    *The Whole World Book of Quotations.*

p. 199    Ibid.

p. 201    Ibid.

p. 209    *Unto Thee I Grant.*

p. 211    Service, Robert. *The Best of Robert Service.* Toronto: McGraw-Hill Ryerson Ltd., 1953.

p. 215    *The Whole World Book of Quotations.*

p. 219    *The Gnostic Gospels.*

p. 221    *Unto Thee I Grant.*

# Bibliography

Braymer, Marjorie. *Atlantis: The Biography of a Legend*. New York: Atheneum, 1983.

Bro, Harmon Hartzel. *A Seer Out of Season: the Life of Edgar Cayce*. New York: Penguin Books, 1989.

Cihlar, Many. *Mystics at Prayer*. 19th ed. San Jose, Calif.: The Rosicrucian Press Ltd., 1982.

Davies, A. Powell. *The Meaning of the Dead Sea Scrolls*. New York: The New American Library Inc. (Mentor Books), 1956.

Donnelly, Ignatius. *Atlantis: the Antediluvian World. A Modern Revised Edition*. Edited by Egerton Sykes. New York: Harper and Brothers, 1949.

Eliot, Charles W., ed. *The Meditations of Marcus Aurelius*. Danbury, Conn.: The Harvard Classics, Groier Enterprises Corp, 1980.

Epictetus. *The Golden Sayings of Epictetus*. Danbury, Conn.: Grolier Enterprises Corp, 1980.

*Holy Bible*. King James translation.

Johnson, Paul. *A History of Christianity*. New York and London: Penguin Books, 1976.

Lewis, H. Spencer. *The Mystical Life of Jesus*. San Jose, Calif.: AMORC, 1937 (reprint 1965).

————. *The Secret Doctrines of Jesus.* San Jose, Calif.: AMORC, 1937 (reprint 1965).

————. *The Symbolic Prophecy of the Great Pyramid.* San Jose, Calif.: AMORC, 1936.

*Legends, Roman Mythology.* Revised ed. New York: Peter Bedrick Books, 1984.

Lucas, Winafred Blake, Ph.D. *Regression Therapy: A handbook for Professionals, Volume 11: Special Instances of Altered State Work.* Crest Park, Calif.: Deep Forest Press, 1993.

Pagels, Elaine. *The Gnostic Gospels.* New York: Vintage Books, 1981.

Petras, Kathryn, and Ross Petras. *The Whole World Book of Quotations: Wisdom from Women and Men around the Globe Throughout the Centuries.* New York: Addison-Wesley, 1995.

Plato. *Dialogues of Plato.* (*Timaeus* and *Critias*). New York: Penguin Books, 1986.

Rampa, T. Lobsang. *The Third Eye, the Autobiography of a Tibetan Lama.* Garden City, N.Y.: Doubleday, 1956.

Service, Robert. *The Best of Robert Service.* Toronto: McGraw-Hill Ryerson Ltd., 1953.

Sri Ramatherin, ed. *Unto Thee I Grant.* 32nd ed. San Jose, Calif.: AMORC, 1979.

Visalli, Gayle, et al. ed. *After Jesus; the Triumph of Christianity.* Pleasantville, N.Y.: Reader's Digest Association, 1992.

Ward, Kaari et al., ed. *Jesus and His Times.* Pleasantville, N.Y.: Reader's Digest Association, 1990.

Zaehner, R. C. *Hinduism.* New York, N.Y.: Oxford University Press, 1966.

# Index

## A

Akashic Records, 170, 203
Alpha level, 31, 35
Ancient mystery schools, 1–2,
    4, 7–8, 16–17, 20, 37, 41,
    198, 204, 213
Angels, 26, 43, 161–173,
    177–178, 183–184,
    187–190, 192–194,
    196–199, 201–204
Astral projection, 201,
    203–209
Auras, 26, 36, 43, 51–52,
    55–57, 59–60, 62–65,
    70–71, 76, 79–80, 82,
    84–85, 94, 101, 165, 180,
    190, 192, 195, 199

## B

Beta level, 31
Buddha, 13–14

## C

Central nervous system, 24,
    140, 159
Chakra energy, 40, 43, 115,
    127, 130, 136–141,
    143–145, 147, 149,
    151–160, 171, 178
Chakra system, 24, 97, 99, 101,
    103, 105, 107, 109, 111,
    113, 115, 117, 119, 121,
    123, 125, 127, 129, 131,
    133, 135–136, 139, 157,
    159, 185, 204
Chakras, 6, 13, 23–24, 43, 48,
    63, 65, 67, 97–100,
    102–107, 110, 114, 117,
    123, 127, 134, 136, 138,
    140–145, 151, 153–160,
    164–165, 169, 171–172,
    177–178, 184, 186–189,
    195, 199, 202, 204–205

—Major, 1–2, 4, 10, 24, 27,
    46–47, 64, 97–99, 102, 110,
    114–115, 117, 127–128,
    131, 134–136, 138, 140,
    142, 144–145, 149,
    151–155, 157, 159–160,
    166

—Minor, 24, 68, 97

—(top to bottom)
    Crown, 6, 37–49, 63–67,
    76, 88, 92–93, 98–101,
    137–139, 141, 143–148,

150–151, 153–158,
164–165, 171, 177–178,
183–186, 188–189,
191–192, 198, 202
Third eye/brow chakra, 6,
23–25, 27–37, 42, 45–46,
48, 65–66, 76, 92–94,
98–101, 139, 141, 144, 146,
148, 150–151, 164–165,
171, 177, 186, 189, 191,
198
Throat, 94, 98–99,
101–102, 107–114, 126,
131, 139, 148–150, 183,
186
Heart, 16, 44, 74–75, 82,
94, 96, 98–99, 114–127,
129, 131, 133, 135, 139,
147–155, 157, 164–165,
171, 175, 177–178, 183,
186, 205, 208, 216
Solar plexus, 98–99,
127–131, 133, 139, 152,
175, 202
Sacral plexus, sexual,
navel, spleen, 98–99, 127,
132–135, 141, 154
Base, earth, root, 38,
98–99, 108–109, 123, 127,
134–140, 143–145, 147,
151–158, 178, 184
— (by number )
Seventh, 100
Sixth, 12, 25, 100
Fifth, 101, 160
Fourth, 114, 162
Third, 23–25, 27–37, 42,
45–46, 48, 65–66, 76, 81,
92–94, 98–101, 121, 127,
130, 139, 141–142, 144,
146, 148, 150–151,
164–165, 171, 177, 186,
189, 191, 198, 208
Second, 28, 32, 37, 40–42,
44, 63, 81, 98, 112, 121,
130–131, 151, 182, 188,
208, 212
First, 29, 32–33, 37, 42, 45,
63, 80–81, 94, 105, 110,
112, 114–116, 120–121,
130, 134–136, 157, 161,
173, 176, 184, 189
Channeling, 9, 161, 163, 165,
167, 169, 171–181,
183–185, 187–191,
193–199
Clairaudient, 36, 42, 48, 164,
187–188
Clairsentient, 42, 48
Clairvoyant, 36, 42, 48, 51, 56,
58, 61, 67, 71–72, 164, 188
Colors of the Aura, 52, 87, 92
Baby pink, 53, 59, 74
Black, 23, 52, 68–71, 84, 182
Bright pink, 68–69, 74
Dark blue, 53, 55–56

Dark green, 68–69, 76
Dirty brown, 73
Dirty orange, 68–69,
72–73
Dirty yellow, 68–69, 71–73
Dull brown, 72
Gold, 52–53, 61–65
Gray, 52, 64, 68–69, 71
Honey or golden brown,
60–61
Light blue, 53–56, 65,
87–88, 185, 192, 206
Light purple, 53, 61–62,
65–66, 76, 98, 100–101
Light to mid green, 53,
56–57, 76–77, 114
Light to mid orange, 53,
61–62, 66–67
Medium to dark red (bur-
gundy), 53, 60
Mid blue, 53–56, 58
Mid purple (indigo),
52–53, 61–62, 65–66, 76,
98, 101
Red, 52–53, 60, 68–69,
74–76, 89–90, 98, 134–135,
184
Reddish purple, 68–69, 76
Silver, 52–53, 62, 64–66, 202
Sunshine or light yellow, 53,
58, 67
White, 6, 19, 51–53, 61–64,
69, 82, 84, 86–89, 105,
146–148, 150, 152–156, 173,
179–180, 185–186, 192–193

**D**

Dharma, 215–216
Divine power, 8–9, 11, 13–15,
100–101, 131, 135–137,
139–141, 144, 154, 156,
162–164, 166, 172–173,
180, 193

**E**

Elohim, 170–171
Empathic, 36, 48, 73, 127, 195
Endocrine glandular system/
endocrine system, 24–25,
35, 47, 97, 102, 108,
114–115, 127, 132, 138,
142, 154, 159–160
Essenes, 10–12, 17

**F**

Frequency, 2, 24, 31, 40–43,
53–56, 58–62, 65–66,
68–69, 98, 100, 169, 172,
178, 189

**G**

Greece, 8, 16

**H**

Healing schools, 2
Heliopolis School, 8–10
Hinduism, 12–14, 100, 211,
213, 215

Human aura/energy field,  2,
9, 24, 41, 43, 51–53, 55,
57–61, 63, 65, 67–73,
75–77, 79–81, 83–85,
87–89, 91, 93, 95, 97–98,
138, 142, 158–159, 164,
178, 185, 190–192
Hypothalamus, 25–26, 38–39,
41–42, 46, 189

**J**

Jesus, 8–12, 14–15, 17, 19, 21,
51, 114, 147, 163, 171, 198,
204, 212–213, 219
Jewish Kabala, 11

**K**

Karma, 215–216
KAYEE, 112
Kundalini, 13, 135, 137–145,
147, 149, 151, 153–157,
159–160

**M**

Magi, 16–17
MAH–RAH, 174–177
MAY, 44–48, 80, 100, 108, 146
Medical lama, 30
Mithra, 17–18
Mithraism, 17, 44
Mother Earth, 20, 85, 134,
144–145, 156, 158

**N**

Near death experience (NDE),
165

**P**

Past life regression, 217
Persia, 8, 14, 16
Pineal gland, 24–25, 27–30,
32–39, 41–42, 46, 101, 148,
150, 189
Pituitary gland, 25, 37–42,
46–48, 100, 189
Possession, 194, 196

**R**

Reincarnation, 13, 170–171,
211–213, 215–217, 219
Roman Empire, 17–18, 212

**S**

Serpent power (see also Kundalini), 3, 135, 137–145,
147, 149, 151, 153–157,
159–160
Spirit guides, 26, 43, 161–162,
164, 166–173, 177–178,
183–185, 187–190,
192–195, 197–199,
201–203
Super learning, 193, 218
Sympathetic nervous division,
24, 137–139, 158–160

**T**

THOH, 31–32, 37, 42, 46, 80, 101

**U**

Universal Energy, 31, 40–41, 43, 81, 103, 107, 138, 141, 145, 165, 202, 208, 214–215

**V**

Vibratory energy, 184, 189, 198

Vibration, 23–24, 28, 30–33, 40–43, 45–46, 51, 53, 55–56, 59, 63–64, 68, 72, 75, 89, 112–113, 115, 131, 145, 159, 163, 169–170, 177, 189, 195

**Z**

Zoroaster, 14–16

# ☽ REACH FOR THE MOON

Llewellyn publishes hundreds of books on your favorite subjects! To get these exciting books, including the ones on the following pages, check your local bookstore or order them directly from Llewellyn.

## ORDER BY PHONE

- Call toll-free within the U.S. and Canada, 1-800-THE MOON
- In Minnesota, call (651) 291-1970
- We accept VISA, MasterCard, and American Express

## ORDER BY MAIL

- Send the full price of your order (MN residents add 7% sales tax) in U.S. funds, plus postage & handling to:

  Llewellyn Worldwide
  P.O. Box 64383, Dept. K214-3
  St. Paul, MN 55164-0383, U.S.A.

## POSTAGE & HANDLING
(For the U.S., Canada, and Mexico)

- $4.00 for orders $15.00 and under
- $5.00 for orders over $15.00
- No charge for orders over $100.00

We ship UPS in the continental United States. We ship standard mail to P.O. boxes. Orders shipped to Alaska, Hawaii, The Virgin Islands, and Puerto Rico are sent first-class mail. Orders shipped to Canada and Mexico are sent surface mail.

International orders: Airmail—add freight equal to price of each book to the total price of order, plus $5.00 for each non-book item (audio tapes, etc.).

Surface mail—Add $1.00 per item.

Allow 2 weeks for delivery on all orders.
Postage and handling rates subject to change.

## DISCOUNTS

We offer a 20% discount to group leaders or agents. You must order a minimum of 5 copies of the same book to get our special quantity price.

---

### FREE CATALOG
Get a free copy of our color catalog, New Worlds of Mind and Spirit. Subscribe for just $10.00 in the United States and Canada ($30.00 overseas, airmail). Many bookstores carry New Worlds—ask for it!

---

Visit our website at www.llewellyn.com for more information.

**CHAKRAS FOR BEGINNERS**
**A Guide to Balancing**
**Your Chakra Energies**
**David Pond**

The chakras are spinning vortexes of energy located just in front of your spine and positioned from the tailbone to the crown of the head. They are a map of your inner world—your relationship to yourself and how you experience energy. They are also the batteries for the various levels of your life energy. The freedom with which energy can flow back and forth between you and the universe correlates directly to your total health and well-being.

Blocks or restrictions in this energy flow expresses itself as disease, discomfort, lack of energy, fear, or an emotional imbalance. By acquainting yourself with the chakra system, how they work and how they should operate optimally, you can perceive your own blocks and restrictions and develop guidelines for relieving entanglements.

The chakras stand out as the most useful model for you to identify how your energy is expressing itself. With *Chakras for Beginners* you will discover what is causing any imbalances, how to bring your energies back into alignment, and how to achieve higher levels of consciousness.

1-56718-537-1, 216 pp., 5 ¾₆ x 8                                        $9.95

**HEALING ALTERNATIVES
FOR BEGINNERS**

**Kay Henrion**

When someone begins to seek out alternative ways of healing, they encounter a deluge of confusing and often conflicting information on health, healing modalities, foods, and supplements, even from the practitioners themselves.

This book, written by a registered nurse, gives people a starting place for their journey into taking responsibility for their own health. It answers questions in layman's language regarding meditation and visualization, diets and vitamins, herbs, homeopathy, therapeutic touch, the aging process, AIDS, even natural healing for pets. It is full of anecdotes and examples from the author's own life and the lives of her patients.

**1-56718-427-8, 264 pp., 5 ³⁄₁₆ x 8**                    **$12.95**